The Economics of Supply
and Demand

The Royer Lectures

Series editor: John M. Letiche, University of
California, Berkeley

First published in Great Britain in 1983 by
Basil Blackwell Publisher Limited
108 Cowley Road, Oxford OX4 1JF, England

First published in the United States of America
in 1983 by The Johns Hopkins University Press,
Baltimore, Maryland 21218

LC 83–48047
ISBN 0–8018–3095–8

Library of Congress Cataloging in Publication Data

Klein, Lawrence Robert.
    The economics of supply and demand
    Includes index.
    1. Supply and demand
    2. Supply-side economics
    3. Keynesian economics. I. Title.
    HB201.K497 1983   338.5$'$21   83-48047

    ISBN 0-8018-3095-8

Typesetting by Unicus Graphics Ltd, Horsham,
West Sussex, England.
Printed in Great Britain by The Pitman Press,
Bath

The Economics of Supply and Demand

Lawrence R. Klein

The John Hopkins University Press
Baltimore, Maryland

Contents

Foreword

Intended for a general as well as a professional audience, this book by Nobel laureate Lawrence R. Klein provides a systematic and original integration of the economics of supply and demand, with related policy implications for worldwide economic readjustment. Much of Professor Klein's theoretical and quantitative research during recent years has been devoted to the substantive issues discussed in this book. He has been concerned with modifying the mainstream macroeconomic model for the analysis of structural complications that arise on a more disaggregated, microeconomic level. These complications are embedded in such cogent supply-side issues as demography, productivity, energy, food, environment, regulation and competitiveness. The synthesis at the core of this book lucidly depicts these macro and micro factors. A succinct Appendix, titled "The Formal Structure of Supply-Side Models" further formulates the principal supply and (postulated) demand relationships for the professional reader.

In delineating the elements of contemporary economic maladjustments, Professor Klein shows that the need for more incisive analysis and operational policies in regard to supply-side economics is to be matched only by that of demand-side economics. The present economic problems of the industrial nations, he observes, are primarily structural: they call mostly for specific, micro policies. Accordingly, supply-oriented analysis requires a microeconomic theory, or model, that can be related to general, or sectoral, microeconomic policy. This, in effect, leads to a method for the integration of supply-side (including structural) relationships and demand-side (overall) relationships. It is a contribution of the first rank to applied economic analysis.

Professor Klein's emphasis on the importance of supply-side economics has practically nothing in common with the "populist" nostrums recently proposed under that name. He builds upon the Leontief model to incorporate relevant, final and intermediate factor-product relationships with input–output coefficients treated as variables, dependent on shifts in relative prices. Demand-oriented systems, he emphasizes, also have to be placed in proper perspective. The Keynesian model became deficient not only because its adherents remained preoccupied with demand, but because it was inherently and necessarily related to macroeconomic policy. It was therefore incapable of dealing with the emergent structural problems. For more satisfactory analysis and relevant policy, Professor Klein coordinates the economics of the supply-side component *via* the microeconomics of the Leontief input–output accounts and the demand-side component *via* the *mainstream* macroeconomics of the national income and product accounts. He goes on to outline the forms in which these accounts can, and should, be coordinated with the flow-of-funds accounts, including the international sector.

This approach, associated with the work of Professor Klein and his associates on the well-known Project LINK, is advanced with admirable balance and proportion. The system is not decomposable. It does not generally admit of a solution to either the supply or demand sides separately. As Professor Klein states: "Both must be solved together" (p. 50). He cautions that the method requires full balance in measures to affect the main aggregates through fiscal spending, taxation, and monetary control. Under contemporary conditions, in his view, policies directed along these lines cannot themselves be expected to bring modern economies into equilibrium. They will have to be supplemented with structural programs to cope with such issues as the maldistribution of unemployment, the imbalance between productivity and real wages, and the disequilibria in agriculture and foreign trade.

The 1981 Royer Lectures delivered by Professor Klein at the University of California, Berkeley, form the basis of this book. Chapters 1–3 comprise the lectures themselves. Chapters 4 and 5 are illustrative, designed to supplement the theory of supply-side modeling, and to illustrate the simulations of the worldwide impact of oil-price increases as an exercise in supply-side economics. Chapters 6–8 are provocatively controversial. With several important exceptions, in Chapter 6 the tenets of monetarism, rational expectations, and "populist" supply-side economics are disputed. Chapter 7 appraises the state of the arts as to economic laws; and Chapter 8 concludes the volume by summarizing the author's analytical interpretations and their policy implications. Both general and professional readers should find the arguments and controversies as set forth here highly illuminating.

We hope the reader will have occasion to share in our gratitude for Professor Klein's timely contribution and our pride in its publication.

Preface

It was an important personal occasion for me to stroll again in the groves where I began my academic career. I felt honored to be giving the Royer Lectures at the University of California before many of my old teachers of forty years ago. But sentimentality aside, the real attraction of giving the Royer Lectures was the opportunity to meet with a scholarly community for a serious discussion of issues associated with supply side economics.

The popular fascination with the concepts of the supply side has found a good reception in the media and politics. The issues are deep and complicated, much too difficult to be treated lightly as is inevitable in those arenas. Unfortunately, "half-baked" ideas have been translated into economic policy without the proper and necessary scholarly investigations. They have had important consequences for our daily lives. By now, the autumn of 1982, this has turned into disappointment and reconsideration of hasty decisions.

There is a very important and sound area associated with theory and policy from the supply side. That area was the focus of scientific exploration that I attempted to emphasize in the Royer Lectures. Much of the ground involves familiar concepts and analysis of academic economics, but I tried to put it together, with well-known analysis from the demand side, in a system of thought that covers the economy as a whole. Naturally, I looked at the subject from a point of view that would be compatible with contemporary macroeconometrics. It is also only natural that a misleading and unbalanced picture would be given from the supply side alone, hence the title of this volume and the attempt to show both sides together — supply and demand, an expression that is as familiar as any other to professional economists.

The lectures proper comprise only three chapters of this volume. In the space of three lectures, it is difficult to cover, page-by-page, material that would fill a book. I, therefore, rounded out the Royer Lectures, as such, with related material. This consists of an equation-outline of the complete supply–demand model that I have in mind; a lecture that I presented to the American Academy of Arts and Sciences in 1982 on Economic Laws; the Suntory–Toyota Lecture that I gave at the London School of Economics, one year later, in which I placed the discussion of supply side economics in the context of challenges to the Keynesian paradigm; and a study that I carried out with some of my associates on the effect of changes in oil prices on the world economy. All these additional materials, some of which have never been published before, are closely related to the subject matter of the Royer Lectures.

As ever, I am indebted to my assistants and associates who faithfully supply me with the necessary back-up materials. I am pleased to have Victor Filatov, Shahrokh Fardoust, and Vincent Su, who have all toiled with me on Project LINK, as co-authors of chapter 5. But most of all, I am indebted to John Letiche, who counseled me on the lectures, the selection of essays for this volume, and the content of the written chapters. His keen eye saved me from many pitfalls.

1 Introduction

Supply and Demand Side Economics: Why the Distinction?

The "law of supply and demand" is so much a part of our subject that it seems unnatural to draw a distinction between demand side economics and supply side economics. Also, Alfred Marshall reminded us that both blades of the scissors do the cutting, and that neither supply analysis alone nor demand analysis alone will provide an adequate explanation of what is happening in the economy. In reality, there ought to be simply a concept of economics that would naturally encompass both supply and demand relations, culminating in the "law of supply and demand" as a market-clearing mechanism to determine prices. This seems obvious enough to professional economists, but popular political discussions have emphasized the newness of supply side economics. I therefore propose to take a good look into the meaning of this notion.

If modern thinking about the supply side of the economy has been developed as the antithesis of demand management from the perspective of demand-oriented systems, we may gain some insight into the meaning of supply side economics by paying some attention first to demand side economics.

The Demand Side

Predominant thinking about the economy as a whole — the macro-economy — is based on the development of Keynesian economics in the 1930s and its widespread use during the entire era after World War II. The Keynesian theoretical system and its public policy implementation were developed to meet the needs of the times – to deal with the worldwide Great Depression of the 1930s. That economic disaster was characterized as a situation of massive lack of "effective" demand. Unemployment, excess capacity, falling prices, low interest rates, and mass poverty all coexisted during this period. The imbalance between potential supply and effective demand was so great that emphasis was placed entirely on demand conditions, the thinking being that supply side issues would accommodate any increases in demand without complication. Little thought was given to the possibilities of inflation, high interest rates, or material shortages in a situation of excess supply or deficient demand. By and large, this was a good way of looking at the situation. The only issue was, for how long? As will be argued below, a point was reached when the conditions of the 1930s no longer prevailed.

Keynesian economics were focused on interpreting and improving a world of deficient demand, but the demand orientation of the system of thought was based on the functioning of the (mathematical) model of the system. The definition of total production from the side of demand emphasizes this:

$$C + I + G + E - M = Y$$

where
C = consumer *demand*
I = investment *demand*
G = public *demand*
$E - M$ = net foreign *demand* (exports minus imports)
Y = gross national product – total demand.

Total demand is determined (analyzed) by determining (analyzing) each component and adding them up to get the total. This is loosely called "aggregate demand analysis." (Keynes also, however, introduced a concept of aggregate supply.) It overlooks the fact that demand for I contributes to capital input in the production-supply process. A part of I, to ensure the satisfaction of the identity, is inventory investment. This component is not wholly demanded. At least some part of inventory investment represents an imbalance between supply and demand. Inventory investment then becomes a buffer between the two. Careful economic analysis would, therefore, recognize fully that many supply aspects enter the Keynesian system. It is predominantly an analysis of demand, especially effective demand; but it is not a pure concept, with both supply and demand considerations being brought to bear on most high-level economic decisions.

Accompanying the Keynesian theory about the functioning of a macroeconomy was a body of knowledge about economic policy. Operating through instruments that public officials have at their disposal for controlling the economy, the intuitive line of policy would be called "demand management." The essential feature of this brand of economic policy is its emphasis on fine-tuning the economy through decision-making about instruments of *macro*-econometrics. The emphasis here is on *macro*.

It is not my purpose here to appraise the theoretical concept of demand-oriented systems or the applications of the principles of demand management to the formulation of economic policy. There will, eventually, be economic historians who will look at the period, roughly between 1930 and 1970, with the objectivity of detached hindsight and place the era of demand economics in its proper historical perspective. In his Yrjö Jahnsson Lectures, entitled *The Crisis in Keynesian Economics*, Sir John Hicks reckoned the third quarter of the twentieth century to be the age of Keynes.[1] This agrees roughly with the analysis that I am about to unfold – namely, that the analysis of supply must be brought to bear more importantly, together with demand analysis, in the formulation of an economic policy adequate to deal with the problems of our times. For me, the end of the 1960s will mark the end of the era that I have in mind as one in which the problems lent themselves well to demand-oriented analysis. The joint theory of supply and demand was always there – available – but it was partially neglected because the emphasis was always on the demand side as far as policy was concerned.

When the economic historians have made their detached studies, they will, I believe, conclude that the policies of demand management, for all their faults and deficiencies, served us well. These policies began to have some impact in the latter part of the 1930s, and the advent of World War II brought about a wholly new

---

[1] John Hicks, *The Crisis in Keynesian Economics* (Oxford: Basil Blackwell, 1974), 1.

economic situation, in which full employment and full capacity utilization were attained by virtue of the world's running a full-scale war economy. But the war did not change the problem permanently. In the period of recovery – most of the decade of the 1950s – and in the period of rapid expansion – the decade of the 1960s – demand management served us well. The main economies of the world experienced only moderate cyclical set-backs on a path of strong expansion. By and large, the 1950s and 1960s were decades of enormous economic improvement and a relapse towards the conditions of the 1930s was avoided, thanks to the judicious application of the techniques of demand management.

In the United States, the tax policies of the Kennedy–Johnson administrations gave us the investment tax credit, liberalized depreciation guidelines, and the income tax cut of 1964. These were all positive policies that did the US economy much good. The excise tax cuts of 1965 pushed a good thing a bit too far and ran into the burgeoning war in Vietnam. From 1965 on, trouble began to build up for the United States. By the end of the decade, the Bretton Woods agreements had run their course of usefulness and had to be abandoned; resource limitations came to the fore; and inflationary pressures mounted. The decade of the 1970s was a turbulent economic period, in which food, fuel, and other limited resources played prominent roles in changing the underlying economic situation. In addition, there were new demographic issues, the ending of the war in Vietnam, the Iranian revolution, the decline of productivity growth, and the other new conditions that surfaced, calling for a fresh approach in both analytical modeling and the formulation of adequate policies. It was a transitional decade. As the 1980s unfold, there will be a new approach in economics to deal with the changed economic circumstances.

In many respects, the success of demand-management policies made them obsolete, but they were also affected by a number of natural and man-made shocks from outside the present mainstream of domestic economic affairs. Had economic policy-makers responded in an adaptive way to these new challenges, they might have achieved a more acceptable economic doctrine and a far better economic situation. In fact, there has been a strong tendency to stay with the same body of economic thought and policy, past the time that obsolescence set in, and the economic situation consequently deteriorated, causing critics to search for a more drastic revision of theory than would otherwise have been called for. In point of fact, we appear all over the world to be locked into a state of stagflation from which conventional demand-oriented macroeconomic analysis offers little hope of extrication. I do not believe that policies to cure stagflation necessarily call for a complete upheaval in economic analysis, but rather that solutions can be found within the framework of existing theoretical knowledge that requires building an appropriate full supply side on to prevailing systems of demand orientation.

In the present situation of stagflation, we cannot return to conventional fiscal and monetary stimuli to deal with the "stag" part, because that runs the danger of stimulating the "-flation" part in an adverse way. By the same token, we cannot turn to the usual macro-methods of stopping inflation through fiscal and monetary policies working together.

A fresh adaptation of existing economic analysis ought to be adequate to the test, but it will not be purely a macro-approach. Associated with the concepts of supply and demand side economics there is also an important distinction between micro- and macroeconomics. A careful consideration of present problems suggests that much is left undone if policy-makers stick closely to macro-policies introduced as broad fiscal measures, broad monetary measures, or overall commercial policy. Macro-policy is best served by these conventional considerations. If we take the view, as will be argued below, that broad policies are not appropriate for the kind of structural issues that have come to the fore during the 1970s, then we shall find that we need a microeconomic theory or model to generate microeconomic policy. A great part of supply side modeling will be recognized as microeconomics. Thus, the total debate will encompass both micro- and macro-considerations, as well as supply–demand considerations.

A New Approach

Instead of looking for finely tuned combinations of macroeconomic policies in the monetary, fiscal, and commercial (trade) areas, attention is now directed towards comprehensive policies that attempt to deal with a variety of structural problems. The end result is stagflation, but the problems that bring this situation about are many and must be attacked from many sides as structural or microeconomic policies, not to the exclusion of macroeconomic policies, but complementary to them. First, it is necessary to delineate the problem areas. Broadly speaking, they are:

  (i) demography
 (ii) productivity
(iii) energy
 (iv) regulation
  (v) environment
 (vi) food.

Demography has been a problem area for several reasons. The most notable problem of the 1970s was to absorb the "baby boom" generation into the work-force. Earlier, there had been a significant expansion of the educational system to absorb these large numbers of pupils. After the population bulge passed through the educational system one elementary or high school after another was closed down, and many institutions of higher learning found themselves in serious financial straits. This required adjustment and rearrangement. Highly educated teachers had to be reoriented. When the baby boom cohort finally entered the work-force, they swelled the ranks of unemployed youths and contributed to an overall lowering of productivity.

At the same time that young people were swelling the labor force, women of many age groups were entering it. They did not necessarily have direct adverse effects on productivity, but they did make the attainment of full employment harder to achieve. In part, the problem was handled by redefining "full employment," but it was not entirely a matter of defining away the problem, because the entrance of women and many young persons into the labor force meant that many family units had multiple earners; hence modest rates of unemployment, above the historic full employment norm of 4.0 percent unemployment, were not as hard to bear during the 1970s as during earlier decades.

Finally, there were problems of national demographic distribution, especially the tug-of-war between the north-eastern and north-central states versus the Sun Belt. This left some northern areas distressed, impoverished, and in need of capital modernization.

Here we have youth unemployment, general unemployment (without some of the hardships) brought about by rapid labor force expansion, and a changing regional composition. How do we deal with these issues? Running a fast or slow economy through overall controls on fiscal and monetary measures will have slight impact on these matters. They represent maladjustments and a great deal of waiting. If we wait long enough, we may see a gradual settling down to a more regular pattern of age distribution towards the bottom end of the range. The prominence of the "baby boom" generation will fade, and gradually they will be absorbed into the normal work pattern with respectable productivity performance. There will still be a problem of youth unemployment, but it will perhaps not be so striking.

A typical policy approach to the youth unemployment problem is to suggest the lowering of the minimum wage rate, at least for a "youth differential." This is a typical example of a microeconomic or structural policy that gets right to the heart of the issue and appears to be better for this problem than general fiscal/monetary policy. The sunbelt distribution problem involves either an acceptance of the desire of people to relocate, or trying to use selective industry subsidies or regional subsidies to slow or halt the continuing trends toward regional redistribution.

The demographic problems are real and of great significance, but they argue for specific tailored policies and not the macropolicies as they would be applied to the overall economy.

Faltering productivity growth, even declining at times, appears to be at the heart of the issue. Vigorous productivity growth is needed if we are to be able to pass steadily improving economic life on to our children. Productivity is important because of the approximate relation:

percentage change in price level
$$= \text{percentage change in unit cost minus}$$
$$\text{percentage change in productivity.}$$

This is a powerful relationship and indicates that if productivity growth can be resumed, it offsets the inflationary content of wage or other unit cost increases. Productivity is important in its own right as well as in contributing to the fight against inflation.

As far as economic policy is concerned, we should be favoring seemingly minor aspects of policy to obtain greater support for productivity growth – increasing the speed on some assembly lines, providing for special skill training of young workers just beginning their careers, support for R & D, for basic research, or for more intensive investment efforts.

Energy cost increases have set back productivity growth, while capacity is being made more energy-efficient. They have also disturbed prevailing life styles, thrown international payments balances into disarray, and generally slowed industry growth. The use of conventional macroeconomic policy, especially monetary policy, to fight the energy problems of 1974–75 proved to be disastrous – enough to put the whole industrial world through a severe recession-cum-inflation.

That energy problems are widely pervasive economic problems is self-evident, but how can they be dealt with from the viewpoint of economic policy? To do so calls from pricing policy, indirect tax policy, windfall tax policy, rationing of fair shares during a potential emergency, creation of massive storage facilities, programs for development of synthetic fuels, environmental protection, and many other policies. None of these is a macro-policy. Each is structurally suited to specific aspects of the energy situation.

Energy issues provide striking examples of demand and supply side economics. Energy conservation issues are fundamentally associated with restraint of demand. That is one side of the energy economy. Enhancement of energy supply is on the other side. Some people favor conservation; some favor supply enhancement; and others look to both sides for economic progress.

Regulation again reduces to a productivity issue. Industry and commerce are regulated, presumably in the public interest to protect health, safety (worker and other), and environmental beauty. There is a feeling that the United States has gone far in regulation. Standards are set too high; regulations are sometimes mutually inconsistent. Compliance slows the work effort and adds to costs, thereby causing more inflation. Most acts of deregulation would appear to cut costs and help in the fight against inflation, but energy deregulation, for example, will in the first instance lead to higher prices. Eventually, prices may decline a great deal after an initial cost-push rise.

Regulation does much good; some of it is absolutely necessary. Deregulation must therefore be selective and judicious. This forces a structural analysis of the problems and is surely not accomplished at a macro-level of abstraction.

The environment is protected by regulation, which is also closely associated with energy issues. The search for oil substitutes may exhaust water supplies or scar the earth's surface (strip mining). The drive for greater coal use can have profound effects on the atmosphere which must therefore be protected, although in a way that does not add inordinate amounts to the cost base.

Environment extends to the more general concept of quality of life, including congestion, provision of social services, traffic, and many other things besides water, air, solid waste, and topology, which are usually associated with environmental protection. Dealing with environmental problems can hardly be accomplished by macro-policies. Overall taxes, spending, and financial market rates have bearings on the state of the environment, but they are not determining. Specific regulations, specific taxes, specific subsidies are all part of microeconomic structural policies that affect environmental affairs. Also, this is the point at which policy-makers must consider interrelationships and side effects. As indicated above, a policy to increase coal use will upset atmospheric cleanliness and call for an associated environmental policy.

Food policy might generally be thought of as one of deregulation at the present time. In keeping with the overall mood of deregulation, the agricultural sector wants to be able to take advantage of deficiencies in world supply that can be met from US sources — either current production or draw-down of stocks. But food appeared as a special world and national economic issue of primary importance at about the same time as fuel. The massive Soviet grain purchases of 1972–73 depleted the US stockpile just prior to the oil embargo; so we readily associate one aspect of inflation with run-ups of food prices and fuel prices as occurred on some occasions during the 1970s.

As far as the United States is concerned, food is a problem area not so much because of domestic conditions as because of world conditions. Agricultural commodities are traded on world markets and follow world price trends. High prices bring forth larger supplies, and there is no longer the fear of overproduction that prevailed during the 1930s, because world demand has increased so much as a result of population growth and upgrading of diets.

Food prices have, on many occasions, been instrumental in sparking rounds of inflation. It is, therefore, not simply a matter of deregulation to allow suppliers to maximize profits, but also one of serving non-farm consumers, as well as foreign policy. The much maligned embargo on grain shipments to the Soviet Union by President Carter was one of the smartest policy decisions that he made, possibly not because of the original intent, but because of the way things worked out in the 1980 season − particularly, the poor crops in the USSR and the United States. Both worked in a direction that justified and validated his policy, for economic reasons that are nowhere to be found in the teachings of macro-economic policy, demand-oriented or otherwise.

These are the ingredients and motivating factors for supply side policies as I interpret that term. There is, however, an entirely different meaning given to the concept. I shall label this the "populist view." It is exemplified by the bold approach to tax cuts known as the Kemp–Roth proposal and the concept of the Laffer curve. The policy prescriptions for large, repeated, and bold tax reductions on an even percentage basis across all income classes (10 percent per year for three years) are based on novel suppositions. The populist view is that federal deficits are caused by recession, and that anti-recessionary policies of the federal government, if bold enough, will stimulate the economy to such a good recovery path that tax collections will rise enough to wipe out the deficit. It is also argued that induced transfer payments will be significantly decreased according to the relationship that makes such payments a direct function of income/activity levels. As the economy went into recession during 1980, tax receipts fell drastically and transfers increased (as did government interest payments); these movements were responsible for the large deficit.

The argument that tax receipts are increased by tax cuts is not new. It was debated hotly on the eve of the tax cuts of 1964. Kemp–Roth advocates point to the success of the 1964 tax cut to show how the deficit was soon reduced as a result of the higher incomes in the broader economy.

Another aspect of the supply side of tax cuts is that members of the work-force should applaud the tax rate reduction to such an extent that they will be enthusiastic about working harder. This feature should increase job respect and motivation to the point at which productivity will be sharply turned around. In technical terms, the populists look for a large and sensitive reaction coefficient, showing response of effort to improved after-tax real-wage income. This is a novel point of view and could be important if it were true. It is not a question of saying straightaway that the populist proposition is wrong; it is simply that such a reaction pattern has not been established – has not been brought before critical professional opinion. There are reasons to question whether there is necessarily a big surge in effort following a tax cut. The coefficient could go either way. The normal pattern would be for effort to be greater as tax brackets are lowered by the 10 percent factor, but there is another powerful concept in economics, called the backward-bending supply curve of labor. This view holds that, after a point has been reached where the wage rate is above the median position, people may *reduce* their effort because they have such large increments that they can well afford to take some added time away from work. It is not yet known which effect will prevail, but we should be prepared to find a mixed case that could go in either direction.

For the populists, supply side economics is presently interpreted as showing the need for tax cuts in order to stimulate effort and productivity. They have a point in arguing that marginal tax rates have become oppressively high in the United States, but there is every reason to doubt that the effort response will be as fast or as large as they anticipate. There is also much reason to doubt that large-scale tax cuts will lead to public sector surpluses (or reduced deficit). Supply side economics would be very thin if it were concerned mainly or entirely with reactions to the tax system. There are also the whole matter of inter-industry relationships, the degree of modernization of capital, the flow of R & D, the amount of basic research, and many other supply side phenomena.

The focus in this discussion has been almost entirely on domestic economic affairs. Occasionally there has been reference to balance of payments problems, stemming from oil price increases and other disturbances in the world economy. But much of supply side economics is concerned with the US trade position and ways of improving net exports.

The economic and geopolitical worlds have changed greatly since the days of dollar shortage and the pervasive supremacy of the United States. On a fairly regular and persistent basis, the

American external position deteriorated; the dollar became weaker; and the competitive edge of the United States fell drastically. Domestic inflation and faltering productivity growth contributed to the competitive decline of the United States. Our share of world trade fell overall and in many important product lines. Additionally, US goods were surpassed in quality in many fields. In areas where we used to be net exporters, we became net importers. When we faced the escalation of energy prices, our trade position deteriorated even more, because the few lines in which we had a comparative advantage were not large enough in volume to compensate for oil bill increases, losses in other export markets, and shifts to imports. Agriculture has remained a strong point, as have jet aircraft, semi-conductors, computers, and invisibles. Given the vast depreciation of the dollar over a number of years, US exports improved greatly and the current account is now in surplus, while the trade account is in deficit.

It is important for the United States as the issuer of a key currency in the world monetary system to try to maintain a stable dollar. We therefore need to have strong external accounts. At the moment, we have good balance, but that position is fragile, and we cannot relax our objectives to rebuild the competitive edge of US exports in world markets. Nor can we draw back from attempting to reduce imports by effectively producing more economically, either in energy or in other lines. These are the roles of the foreign accounts in supply side economics.

Summary

This introductory statement can be summarized as follows. Demand management as a policy that follows from demand-oriented theoretical systems is to be put in its proper perspective. It has done much good, in taking off from the problems of the 1930s and the early postwar economy, but it is not adequate to meet the problems of today, especially those that apparently lie ahead for the decade of the 1980s. It is not only a preoccupation with demand that makes this approach deficient; it is mainly a preoccupation with *macro*-policy.

A listing of the issues of today clearly brings out the fact that present problems are structural, not macro, or overall. They require specific policies, some micro-policies, and many decisions that are based on supply-oriented analysis. Supply side economics, in the present understanding, deals with demography, productivity, energy, regulation, environment, and food. This list is not exhaustive, but it is comprehensive.

The view of supply side economics being put forward here differs markedly from the populist view that equates supply side analysis with general tax cuts, very close to those that are usually advocated by proponents of macro-demand management. The populist view is based not on critical empirical tests, but on the assumption or hypothesis that the marginal tax rates stifle incentives to the point at which their (tax) liberalization may be expected to unleash large amounts of pent-up energy that will raise productivity by significant amounts.

Finally, some international considerations are introduced into the discussion. Generally speaking, America seems to have lost her competitive edge. This unsettles the trade accounts, weakens the dollar, contributes to inflation, and encourages the introduction of trade restrictions. For these reasons, export promotion and conservation appear to offer the best chance for success in overcoming our "energy" shortfalls.

2 Implementing Supply Side Policies

In order to appreciate and understand the newer supply side policies from the point of view of their implementation, I shall first review the same issues on the more familiar demand side.

An important distinction for such policies has been the separation into discretionary or judgmental policy actions versus fixed rules. The latter have been emphasized to a large extent by Milton Friedman, who would like to tie money supply growth and public expenditure growth to the growth of the nominal GNP. These may or may not be good rules, but it is one thing to argue in their favor as components of macro-policy and another to make them central and dominant, that is, to have these two and other very simple rules, with the market doing the rest of the allocation job.

Examples of discretionary policy are the usual counter-cyclical proposals for money supply, public spending, public revenues (taxation), and external commercial policy to "lean against the wind" – to restrain the economy when it appears to be growing too strongly and generating inflationary pressures or to stimulate the economy when it appears to be growing too slowly, without visible inflationary pressure.

Without imposing such simple rules as the Friedmanesque criteria for money supply and public spending growth, we can still formulate *automatic* policy along the lines suggested by A. W. Phillips.[1] Public expenditures are activated or restrained on the

---

[1] A. W. Phillips, "Stabilization Policy in a Closed Economy," *Economic Journal* 64 (June 1954): 290–323.

basis of shortfalls or overshoots of real GNP targets by combinations of level, derivative, and integral rules. These are corrective devices that are traditionally employed in stabilizing engineering systems. From the point of view of the present discussion, the main feature of interest is their automatic character. They are more complicated than Friedmanesque rules; nevertheless, they are automatic, working through the principles of demand management. Another type of automatic device, which is already built into the system, is the automatic, or built-in, stabilizer. Such devices are exemplified by the progressive income tax, unemployment compensation, bank deposit insurance, and a number of other protective measures that we implemented in the United states after the bad experience of the 1930s. They are activated in "hard times" to stimulate the economy, and they also choke off expansion automatically. This is especially true of the progressive income tax, which creates "fiscal drag" as a counterweight to expansion.

Some statistical characteristics and implications of the working of the stabilizers can be seen in Table 1, interpreted by the note that accompanies it.

The macroeconomic policy process in the United States works differently in practice from the textbook descriptions that imply that policy-makers can turn on or turn off stimulus on short notice. In fact, the process is cumbersome and slow. often so awkward that its purposes can be readily defeated. The strongest argument for automatic policies is that they do not require tortuous proposing, argumentation, and voting at each stage; they supposedly go into effect immediately. The built-in stabilizers do their work silently and have, indeed, contributed a great deal to the large amount of economic stability that was realized between 1946 and 1973. The fluctuations in disposable income, for example, were much more moderate than those in GNP. Possibly, the progressivity of the personal tax system was pushed too far – such is the contention of the populist school of supply side policy advocates – but that is not the fault of the automaticity; it is the fault of the policy proposers.

Strict rules have not been accepted in the United States, although it has often been suggested that they be adopted. All policies, whether discretionary or for installation of rules, must go through the proposal review process of the federal administration and both

Table 1 Some economic indicators

	Real GNP (1972 US $ billions)	Real GNP (% change)	Real disposable income (1972 US $ billions)	Transfers to persons (US $ billions)	Unemployment (%)
1950	534.8	8.7	362.9	14.4	5.3
1951	579.4	8.3	372.7	11.6	3.3
1952	600.8	3.7	383.2	12.1	3.0
1953	623.6	3.8	399.1	12.9	2.9
1954	616.1	−1.2	403.3	15.1	5.5
1955	657.5	6.7	426.9	16.2	4.4
1956	671.6	2.1	446.3	17.3	4.1
1957	683.8	1.8	455.6	20.1	4.3
1958	680.9	−0.4	460.7	24.3	6.8
1959	721.7	6.0	479.7	25.2	5.5
1960	737.2	2.2	489.7	27.0	5.5
1961	756.5	2.6	503.8	30.8	6.7
1962	800.3	5.8	524.9	31.6	5.5
1963	832.5	4.0	542.3	33.4	5.7
1964	876.4	5.3	580.8	34.8	5.2
1965	929.3	6.0	616.3	37.6	4.5
1966	984.8	6.0	646.8	41.6	3.8
1967	1011.4	2.7	673.5	49.5	3.8
1968	1058.1	4.6	701.3	56.4	3.6
1969	1087.6	2.8	722.5	62.8	3.5
1970	1085.6	−0.2	751.6	76.1	4.9
1971	1122.4	3.4	779.2	90.0	5.9
1972	1185.9	5.7	810.3	99.8	5.6
1973	1255.0	5.8	865.3	114.0	4.9
1974	1248.0	−0.6	858.4	135.4	5.6
1975	1233.9	−1.1	875.8	170.9	8.5
1976	1300.4	5.4	907.4	186.4	7.7
1977	1371.7	5.5	939.8	199.3	7.0
1978	1436.9	4.8	981.5	214.6	6.0
1979	1483.0	3.2	1011.5	239.9	5.8
1980	1480.7	−0.2	1017.7	284.0	7.1

Note: Real GNP falls in recession years, 1953–54, 1957–58, 1969–70, 1973–75, 1979–80, but real disposable income does not fall in those periods, except from 1973 to 1974. In all other downturns it continues to rise, largely as a result of increased transfer payments from the public sector to private persons. Transfers (unadjusted for inflation) make significant jumps whenever real GNP falls. Jumps might occur in other periods, too, for a variety of reasons. In some cases, transfers were indexed upward; for others they were distributed on a broader, more liberal, basis. The right-hand column shows the unemployment rate, which increases significantly when real GNP falls. At the same time, it can be seen that transfers rise markedly when the unemployment rate rises; a good portion of the transfers consist of unemployment benefits.

houses of Congress. Public hearings, committee reports, voting, reconciliation of Senate/House differences – all with a great deal of lobbying in between – are very time-consuming. It took President Johnson two years, ending in 1968, to get a tax surcharge expenditure limitation bill through Congress to pay for the Vietnam War. The delay, in itself, did much damage to the effectiveness of the ultimate legislation. Monetary policy can be altered faster by the Federal Reserve System, but it, unfortunately, cannot carry the whole policy burden by itself and also takes long lead times to be effective.

The statutory independence of the Federal Reserve System, which makes for the flexibility of its actions, is not complete in practice. It must expose its policies to the public scrutiny of Congress, as a result of the provisions of the Humphrey–Hawkins bill, and its chairman is subject to presidential selection (with Senate confirmation) every four years.

To speed up the policy process, the executive branch has, on occasion, asked for discretionary authority to move income tax bracket rates upwards or downwards by limited amounts in order to implement tax policy more expeditiously. This authority has not been granted by a jealous Congress, which guards the origination of money bills in the House via the Ways and Means Committee.

In summary, demand management is vigorously applied, but with less than total smoothness of operation. It is principally subject to serious time delays. These remarks are appropriate for domestic policy, but international economic policy is becoming more important. Here implementation gives rise to some entirely different issues.

The most important international policies concern the setting of tariffs or equivalent non-tariff barriers to trade, and the stabilizing of exchange rate movements. Specific tariffs on individual lines of goods – shoes, textiles, TV sets, cameras, steel, and the like – are not macro-policies. The average level of tariffs across all goods, and general movements towards liberalization, as in the Kennedy Rounds and Tokyo Round, are essentially macro-policies. In this respect, the process is mixed. The president has some personal authority to effect tariff rates, but Congress must vote on something as comprehensive as the Tokyo Round.

As for direct policy intervention to support the dollar, that is a matter under control of the Federal Reserve in open market or central bank swap operations and of the Treasury for gold sales. But the complicated set of factors that influence capital markets and exchange rates are the outcomes of overall policy-making in the total economic environment.

Implementation of Supply Side Policies

As I tried to clarify in Chapter 1, supply side policies deal with structural characteristics of the economy and the various ailments that have arisen in connection with them — demography, productivity, energy, regulation, environment, and food. These are not exhaustive, but they are important and indicative.

Let us first look at some supply side policies connected with these issues and consider the problems of their implementation. A striking demographic issue is the existence of youth unemployment. It may be a question of black and urban area unemployment, too. This is a perplexing and serious problem whose resolution is not fully understood, yet it is surmised by many economists that it would be alleviated if there could be some relaxation of minimum wage legislation. As I suggested in Chapter 1, the increments should be rolled back or a youth differential should be introduced. This is a typical structural policy, not a macro-policy. It might well be called a supply side policy. It seems to me that it is well worth a try, but even if the executive branch wanted to introduce it, there would be strong congressional opposition. This opposition may be based on independent thinking that a mark of social progress in a rich country is its ability to raise standards at the bottom of the scale. It may also be knee-jerk reaction based on thinking that was relevant some decades ago, when the minimum was truly near or below human subsistence and poverty was more widespread. The entire source of opposition comes not from Congress, but from the trade union movement, which influences Congress. In the end, it is extremely difficult to implement this supply side policy, which has, in fact, been recommended by economists but not accepted by Congress. Perceiving the degree of congressional opposition, administration officials have been lukewarm.

If there is to be federal support of on-the-job training in the private sector in order to raise productivity, it would be necessary to have some subsidization of wages for young, inexperienced workers. This would affect wage structure, and thereby incurs trade union opposition. It would have to have much stronger and broadly based support than now apparently exists in either Congress or the administration. To me, it seems to be a straightforward, good supply side policy, but its implementation is dubious.

A similar line of opposition or lack of spirited support seems to be associated with the raising of R & D activity in the private sector through federal subsidization. In the interests of budget cutting, starting with President Johnson's tax surcharge and expenditure control act of 1968, the amount of federal support for R & D either in real terms or as a fraction of GNP, was reduced significantly until late in the decade, when a modest upturn got under way. Over a long period of time, such restraint surely took its toll of the innovation process. Overall investment has apparently suffered in a relative sense and specific investment for modernization and technical improvement has also suffered. The appropriate policy seems to be quite evident – namely, renew federal support on an expanding scale. This goes not only for R & D but also for basic research. There are some indications that, with the revival of national defense expansion, in real terms, there will also be more funding available for R & D. Although I am not arguing for military R & D, I recognize that in the past military R & D has spilled over into civilian application. While the new administration may avoid increasing support for R & D, because of its preoccupation with budget cutting, it will surely be sympathetic to expansion on the military side, and Congress will undoubtedly go along with it, too.

The Kemp–Roth tax cuts are across-the-board reductions of personal tax rates, and as such are purely macro-policies, without targeted supply side effect on stimulating investment activity. Fortunately, the administration has coupled the personal tax cuts with a proposal for accelerated depreciation. I would expect the latter tax proposal to improve the level of capital formation and eventually turn into productivity gains, but the Kemp–Roth proposals should have the primary effect of increasing consumer purchasing power and induce more capital formation through improved activity levels. Whether it will directly improve work incentives and raise productivity in that way is more problematical.

On the international side, supply-oriented policies should be associated with a reduction of oil imports and an expansion of exports. These policies should work in favor of continuing dollar strength and, by virtue of that effect, should tend to hold down inflation. During the periods of severe dollar depreciation in 1978–79, it is felt that we added one or two percentage points per year to the inflation rate as a consequence of exchange weakness. The policy should be to have a steady dollar, not a dollar that steadily rises in exchange value nor one that overshoots.

What are the possibilities of our adopting supply side policies that support the net export position and dollar stability? We have already seen the first step in oil price decontrol and may well see a follow-through policy with respect to gas. Those steps are by presidential order, and their implementation has not been difficult so far. Their effects are to encourage energy conservation by making US prices more like those in main partner countries, with the exception of Canada and Mexico. We can already see a reduction in the volume of oil imports under the influence of past price rises, and this process ought to quicken now that total decontrol has been instituted for oil. The new prices should also encourage more exploration and thus increase physical supply. This, too, will hold back imports.

The United States has never successfully established public boards that have encouraged exports on a large scale. Jurisdictional arguments and ineffective powers have led to less than full success, but there is still a reservoir of feeling that much more can be done to encourage and facilitate exports so that gains can be made on that score.

Two particular approaches in connection with discussions of "industrial policy" are under consideration for further expansion of exports. One such approach is the establishment of an American trading company, patterned after the seemingly successful ventures in Japan. Whether we can do this or not is questionable, but it is surely worth a try. As for its implementation, some hurdles have been overcome in a preliminary way. These are the allowance of such a conglomerate under our anti-trust laws and our banking laws. The conglomerate would have to include industrial, shipping, banking, and merchandising components. This new policy thrust is just being put into practice.

The other approach is to try to identify the winning industries of the next era – a decade or so. Microelectronics, fiber optics, information processing, and possibly bioengineering are some that are often mentioned and are being pushed in competitor nations at the present time. It is a matter not only of picking winners, but also of refurbishing industries that have slipped, such as steel, and helping others in which we have a comparative advantage – agriculture and coal. In the case of these natural resources, it is a question of holding our position, even though they are not winners on a world scale for others.

Overall industrial policy, the risky business of picking the winners, and the establishment of a trading company are all potential policy lines. They have not yet been implemented, but they all hold out promise and are under discussion. It appears to me that these are without a doubt supply side policies and have good chances for implementation.

Incomes Policies and Indexation

There is one class of policies that has not been mentioned, but can readily fit into the discussion – that is, incomes policies, or TIPs. To one way of looking at the issues, incomes policies are in the spirit of demand management. It is proposed that the income tax system be used to penalize firms for granting excessive wage increases or imposing excessive price increases, or to reward households and firms for accepting guideline wage or price increases. These appear to be simply macroeconomic manipulations of the tax system to achieve certain inflation targets.

I have previously been associated with a similar proposal, but one that introduces two different features. In the first place, it makes productivity the key control variable, in that wage increases are to be limited to a moving average of productivity gains and the after-tax rate of profit is to move at the same rate as productivity. The corporate tax rate is to be manipulated so as to make the net rate of return on capital conform to the prescribed rate. The tax system, and not an army of controllers, is being relied upon to achieve the goals of the plan. The second feature that makes this an attractive scheme is its fair shares setup. It treats guidelines for profits on the same plane as the guideline for wages. In this way, it has been found possible to gain trade union approval, a necessary step for its implementation.

By tying the performance to productivity, a semblance of supply side economics is introduced, but it is a macro-policy and not fundamentally different from incomes policies in general. Incomes policies do not try to initiate basic structural changes in the economy. They do not attempt to alter the laws of production from the physical side – that is, they do not focus directly on increasing productivity. They attempt mainly to stabilize the dynamics of income distribution. If they have effects on the laws of production, it is mainly through altering market conditions, i.e., the wage–price bargaining process.

If it is concluded that all fundamental structural policies, especially those that go beyond pure macro-demand management, have been implemented to the fullest extent possible within the terms of reference of our present political system, and if it also happens that stagflation has not been properly dealt with, then I believe that we might turn to incomes policies as a last resort. They are simply a systematic procedure for bringing both sides (producers and consumers, employers and employees) to a bargaining situation in which they are not restricted in decision-making to routes that, in theory, fully respect individual profit or utility maximization simply because economists claim these routes to be in society's best interests. From an individualistic point of view, they cannot readily perceive those interests.

We have not properly tried out incomes policies in the United States. The Kennedy–Johnson wage guidelines, the Nixon NEP (New Economic Policy), and the Carter voluntary guidelines were not implemented in a full sense. They were partial rather than comprehensive. They were not integrated with a vision or model of the economy as a whole. They were not always mandatory. Voluntary and partial systems probably will not work.

There is a role and place for incomes policies in our armory of weapons for stabilizing the economy. It is not a central role, but they should be kept in readiness. Another related policy is indexation. The proponents of automatic, as distinct from discretionary, policy are attracted by indexation because it operates by fixed rules. It is sometimes discussed for wage bargaining, for the adjustment of pension benefits, for marketing of fixed income securities, and for the setting of tax rates. If the principles and points of debate are taken seriously, indexing should be comprehensive and not partial – just like an incomes policy.

While indexation has an aspect of social justice in terms of preventing inflation from radically distorting the income distribution, it has many drawbacks. It does not deal with the problem of inflation in any curative way. It validates inflation. It recognizes what has occurred and adjusts for it. It seems to me that it is preferable for "men of reason" to make controlled adjustments in pensioners' incomes and periodic revisions in income tax rates, rather than to build an automatic process into the economy. I say that because I have found that econometric models with indexation tend to be more unstable, in a dynamic sense, than models without indexation, i.e., the more the economy is indexed, the greater becomes the sensitivity of price swings in the system to external shocks. In this sense full indexation tends to be destabilizing.

Public Acceptance

Overall tax cuts are always welcomed by the citizenry at large; so is comprehensive indexation in an inflationary era. The public can probably be persuaded to accept a strictly macro-policy. If supply side economics is understood in the sense in which I have been using the term, however, the associated structural policies will rarely have easy acceptance by the public at large. That is because some group is usually favored at the expense of others or is hurt either absolutely or relatively to others. None the less, these impacts on particular groups are only temporary. The policies are implemented in order to improve the overall functioning of the economy in the medium term.

The mood is not always ripe for new thinking, but people have had enough time to absorb in their thinking the impact of oil shortfalls, of environmental deficiencies, and of structural unemployment. They have seen the continuing failure of conventional macro-policies. It appears to me that the time is ripe for public acceptance of a truly new approach. It will be more micro in character, more targeted, more specific, but, above all, in my opinion, more fundamental.

In trying to convince the public of the importance of accepting this new approach or extension of existing policy lines, it is important not to raise expectations.

(i) Results are likely to be slow – not rapid – in realization.
(ii) Gains from any one policy are likely to be modest, even for coordinated policy as a whole.
(iii) Pinpoint accuracy in stage-by-stage implementation is not likely to be achieved.

A number of good policies that would raise the investment ratio in the GNP by as much as two percentage points – a very large gain – would be expected to add up to one-half a percentage point to the growth rate, to take off about one-half a percentage point from the inflation rate, and to add, at most one full percentage point to the growth rate of productivity. These are not large gains. They are all in the right direction, and they add a great deal to the total GNP (inflation adjusted) through the workings of the laws of compound interest over fairly long stretches of time, but they do not dramatically turn the economy around. They do not bring us back to the "good old days" of annual 4 percent real growth with 4 percent unemployment, 2 percent inflation, and a balanced external sector.

Many such policies – painstakingly implemented to cover enhancement of R & D, encouragement of scientific research, training of workers on the job, motivation to save more, motivation to invest, conservation of energy demand, enhancement of energy supply, protection of the environment, and so on – in full supply side detail could push the gains further, given enough time. This is what the public must be educated to accept. It is realistic, and promises to produce real gains. But such policy approaches must be sold to the public on a sound basis, particularly avoiding overselling in order to avoid the creation of disappointment or loss of credibility along the painful way.

3 The Theory of Supply and Demand Side Economics

An Overview

Broadly speaking, the economy is structured in the following way:

Households		Enterprises
Demand consumer goods	=	Supply consumer goods
Supply labor	=	Demand labor (supply *and* demand for capital goods)

Supply and demand economics are based on the clearing of markets for final goods and production factors in order to determine prices or, to put it another way, to find a set of prices that would clear markets.

This is an extremely simple framework that leaves several things out of account – namely, a public sector, an international sector, the financial sector, asset/liability positions (and their changes), and the supply of money.

Within the enterprise sector, two kinds of goods are produced: consumer goods and producer goods. The former are used by households for final consumption, and they constitute the demand side of the supply–demand relationship for goods. Enterprises also produce goods for other enterprises. Some of these are *intermediate* goods, and need further processing; they will be discussed later, under the heading of "Input–output analysis." But some are *final* goods. They are goods that are used to produce other goods. This flow of goods, internal to the enterprise sector, is called investment

25

or capital formation. This is the meaning of the parenthetic listing under enterprise activity.

Demand-oriented theory emphasizes the role of demand in this layout. It analyzes the demand for goods by households, the demand for labor by enterprises, and the demand for capital goods by enterprises, assuming implicitly that adequate supplies of capital goods will be forthcoming from the business sector. A macro-demand model looks at these demand components for the economy as a whole or large segments of it. A more detailed model that is demand-oriented disaggregates demand for goods – possibly also for factors – into many sub-components, such as types of consumer spending, types of capital goods, types of investors, and possibly types of labor input. Even though such a model may be large and detailed, it may still be a demand-oriented model geared to macro-demand analysis or management through summation of demand for components.

Supply side theory, on the other hand, pays particular attention to labor supply by households, its sensitivity to net factor incomes (after taxes) and some demographic developments. The specification of household reactions to market conditions figures importantly in the populist view of supply side economics. It is, in fact, part of the total demand–supply process, but supplies of other basic resources such as food, fuel, and industrial materials need to be included in an important way if contemporary supply factors of interest are to be brought into the analysis.

If a variety of business costs, degrees of capacity utilization, and supplies of goods in more detail are to be analyzed separately, but within the context of a full system, there would have to be large-scale disaggregation of the enterprise supply relationships. This would be the direction for supply-oriented modeling corresponding to the same kind of disaggregation in demand-oriented modeling.

From an accounting point of view, a complete description of what is going on in the economy needs to have three economywide statements: (i) the national income and product accounts; (ii) the input–output accounts; and (iii) the flow-of-funds accounts. Demand-oriented models stay closely within the confines of the national income and product accounts, using only some price, labor market, and monetary data for supplementary information.

The most important extension is to include the inter-industry flows of goods that make up the input–output accounts. There is a conventional approach to input–output modeling that takes demand as given and computes the associated levels of output. That would appear to be pure supply side analysis. It is not complete on the supply side, but it does include many of the important ingredients.

The most important step in building a complete demand and supply system is to integrate the national income and product accounts with the input–output accounts. This should be done in a full feedback mode, so that the flows of output by sector cannot be determined without knowing the sector-by-sector levels of demand, while at the same time the demand levels by sector cannot be determined without knowing the sectoral outputs.[1]

In my presidential address to the American Economic Association, I called the model that resulted from the combination of the national income and product accounts with the input–output accounts a "Keynes–Leontief model." I meant that the overall performance of the economy, especially the demand performance, would be generated by a Keynesian-type system and that the inter-industrial model would be generated by the Leontief system.

In a superficial sense, the Keynesian component of the combined model represents the demand side, and the Leontief component the supply side. But in a deeper and more comprehensive sense, the Keynesian component needs to be expanded in two dimensions before it is adequately incorporated in this kind of system.

In the first place, if the input–output component has a significant disaggregation, it should contain upwards of 50 or 100 different sectors — rows and columns of the input–output table. The precise size is not a fixed number; it is flexibly determined on the basis of how much detail we, as analysts, want to deal with, or are able to deal with. All such model constructs are approximations to the "true" economy, and various degrees of approximation are possible. To support a given size inter-industry flow system of

---

[1] An empirical representation of such a system is given in R. S. Preston, "The Wharton Long Term Model: Input–Output within the Context of a Macro Forecasting Model," *Econometric Model Performance*, ed. L. R. Klein and E. Burmeister (Philadelphia; University of Pennsylvania Press, 1976) 271–87.

accounts, we need to introduce a number of final demand components. Again, without a fixed rule, I would say that upwards of 40 final demand categories are needed in order to support about 75 inter-industry categories.

The second dimension of expansion of the Keynesian component is the introduction of model relationships that generate the "income" components of the national *income* and product accounts. The Keynesian system is concerned with the explanation of the flow of factor income, as well as with the flow of final demand. An adequate explanation of the flow of factor income is, in fact, the supply side of the Keynesian system. In a purely aggregative sense, these components consist of a production function and the associated relationships of factor demand. They can also be expressed in terms of macro-cost functions or product supply functions. A balancing of supply and demand in the labor market requires the corresponding development of labor supply relationships, which are at the forefront of contemporary discussions of supply side economics.

As in the case of final demand, this kind of analysis cannot be carried out at a grossly aggregative level if it is to be supportive and fully integrated with an inter-industry system of some 75 sectors. In the limit, there should be a set of production–cost relationships for each sector (column) of the input–output table. Lack of data usually forces some compromising combinations, but at least 40 would be needed.

The determination of factor prices, together with factor inputs, enables one to form factor incomes and thus complete the "income" part of the national income and product accounts.

It was noted above that three basic social accounting statements fully describe the functioning of the social accounting needed for establishment of model scope. In a formal sense, the Keynes–Leontief system whose form I have sketched here deals with two of the accounts; the third is the flow-of-funds accounts, which are wanted in order to complete the financial structure of the model economy. The generation of savings and investment flows, in the context of the Keynes–Leontief system, is traditionally combined with a very simple structure – a central monetary authority's choosing either the growth path of money aggregates or a key interest rate. If it is the former, the key rate is determined from a supply–demand relationship for a money aggregate. The whole spectrum of rates is then determined from the term structure of rates.

Within the spirit of the *structural* nature of issues in supply side modeling, it appears preferable, to my way of looking at things, to model the various components of the rate spectrum by supply–demand analysis of individual classes of financial asset instruments, rather than to use the synthetic approach of the term structure. There are peculiar geographical patterns, institutional restrictions, and other distinct features of money market structure that would suggest that it is more fundamental, and therefore better, to model the whole flow of funds, rather than to use the key rate-cum-term structure approach. With banking practice and security markets undergoing such rapid technical change, it is possible that the term structure will undergo shifts and tilts without our being able to see the underlying forces at work. Just as environmental, cost, and resource limitation issues have driven us to delineate the economic conditions of physical supply in our theoretical and empirical models, so the new financial market issues have driven us toward a similar analysis of supply–demand relations in instruments of wealth. That means, to me, the modeling of the flow of funds.

Within my own group – Wharton Econometric Forecasting Associates – we have fully integrated models based on the input-output accounts with models based on the national income and product accounts. We have partially integrated models based on the flow-of-funds accounts with models based on the national income and product accounts. It now remains to complete the circle by bringing all three together. The linking mechanism to integrate the flow-of-funds accounts should eventually be the spectrum of interest rates, for mortgage rates will relate to residential construction, short-term rates to inventory investment, long-term bank rates to fixed investment, and so forth. At present, in the Wharton Model the linkages with the macro-national income account model are effected through wealth variables that are generated by the flow-of-funds system and appear in various capital formation equations of the other system. The flow-of-funds system and the national income and product system are combined in full feedback relationship, although the linking variables are not interest rates.

There is yet an international aspect to be dealt with in this excursion into flow-of-funds accounting. The US economy is now very much an open system. Moreover, we have noticed significant international imbalances and serious repercussions as a result of new supply side conditions, particularly in fuel and food trade. Merchandise trade can be fully reflected in the input–output flows and in the national income and product accounts, but factor income (especially dividends, interest, and retained earnings) is closely associated with financial flows of past periods as well as with contemporary money market rates. There is something new, however, in the present situation – namely, the freeing up of exchange rate movements after the breakdown of the Bretton Woods system. In order to explain the spectrum of exchange rates, in addition to the spectrum of interest rates, it is necessary to be able to model international capital flows, which means the modeling of a complete sector of the flow-of-funds accounts – namely, the international sector.

A consequence of the theoretical approach that I have been outlining is that models and the associated system of relationships must be large and detailed. The simple macro-rules of the abbreviated Keynesian system, as exemplified in the *IS–LM* diagram, or the monetarist system, as exemplified in the quantity equation, are no longer considered very useful, except as indicative pedagogical devices. It means that the back-of-the-envelope approach to economic reasoning is *chose passé*. The kinds of problems that are being faced today, especially in the supply side components, require an analysis of interrelationships among age-specific distributions, industrial sectors, and commodity types. They are not micro in the true Walrasian sense, but they are an order of magnitude different from experience in macroeconomic analysis. With the compact macro-models, we developed associated policies of macro-demand management. Now I am saying that the new generation of supply–demand models supported by the three accounting systems is needed in order to develop associated policies of modern economic management on both the supply and demand sides of the equations. We have moved from the analytical processes of the single-equation monetarist position and the two-equation Keynesian position, to the 1,000-or-more-equation position of modern supply–demand analysis. That is a consequence of the theoretical system that I am outlining.

The electronic computer, data bases, and the modern information system make all this possible. The integrated system of input–output and national income and product accounts that is now used by the Wharton group has 1,500 relationships, apart from the pure input–output relations. This proliferation of size will not continue indefinitely. There are limitations of human capabilities – the mind, the availability of information, and manageability – but further growth is possible. Bigness, in itself, is not the issue. Bigger is not necessarily better. The issue is to construct the theory and the model that are adequate to the task.

This point of view does not imply that all economic analysis must go in this direction. All economists should not become big system manipulators. There are many partial, compact problems that are more properly analyzed in truncated systems by themselves. But the big social problems that require national policy have system-wide effects, with feedback. Energy, food, environment, demographic structure, and the like do need this kind of analysis. The theoretical system that properly incorporates supply side economics needs this large supporting structure. It is my opinion that simplistic monetarism failed in the face of the various crises of 1970–75, and that populist supply side economics will similarly fail. If we are to solve the stagflation problem in a reasonable way, it will be necessary to approach it from the theoretical side that I have been outlining.

The Extended Laws of Production

Paul Douglas developed the laws of production as relationships between value added output and input of labor and capital.[2] Growth theory has used this formulation to a large extent. It can be justified on an economy-wide basis because some outputs of particular sectors are inputs for others. On a net basis, for the economy as a whole, labor and capital are the inputs. If we are to handle energy input problems and also inputs of basic materials other than fuels, this type of production function will not be informative. It is applicable only for the closed system case of the aggregative economy.

[2] P. H. Douglas, "Are There Laws of Production?" *American Economic Review* 38 (1948): 1–41.

The embedding of an input–output table, as I described it in the previous section, should take care of all the details of intermediate input flows, which covers the use of fuel and other basic materials. This is not the end of the matter, however, because input–output systems, even when put in coefficient form, are not arrays of stable coefficients. If we take the more general view, which I believe is essential, we must regard input–output coefficients as variables, changing as market and technical conditions change.

With this view in mind, the laws of production, in the limit, should make gross output (as distinct from value added) dependent on each of several intermediate inputs, labor, and capital. For any given sector, each of these inputs is sector-specific. They are the same as entries along a column for an input–output (I–O) system of accounts. The column entries in the I–O table are thus the intermediate inputs of a production function. Other inputs come from the associated entries of sector-specific national income flows for labor and capital, appropriately deflated by relevant factor prices.

A more practical, but approximate, procedure is to group the intermediate inputs up and down the column of an input–output table into energy or materials at the most aggregative level, or into a few different types of material. The energy types are quite general and adequate for many using industries, but the material types are more specific and have to be considered on a case-by-case basis.

After the oil embargo of 1973 and the subsequent economic concern about the role of energy, the appropriate production relation became the *KLEM* production function, relating gross output to capital, labor, energy, and materials. At an aggregative level, this displaced the relation between value added, on the one hand, and capital and labor on the other. In this way, energy and its substitutability for other factors could be explicitly studied in a model framework.

This may seem like a great advance in macroeconomics, but it has long been familiar in agricultural economics, where production analysis – both theoretical and applied – has considered fertilizer, feed, seed, insecticide, fuel, and irrigation as intermediate inputs in addition to land, labor, and capital, which are all value added inputs.

Since energy is imported into the United States in large quantities, the separate treatment of energy is related to the more extensive problem of separate treatment of imported materials as factor inputs. In developing countries, centrally planned economies, and some industrial countries that lack basic resources, imported materials and fuel are important for production. If they are not available, production is restrained. The aggregative demand model of Keynesian economics views import multipliers as negative. The more a country imports, the more domestic production is displaced. This surely has to be modified to distinguish between imported materials and other imports. It is in this spirit that intermediate inputs such as energy and materials are introduced into the gross production function.

The laws of production establishing relationships between relative factor inputs and relative factor prices can then be developed together with the *KLEM* production function. This gives a basis for treating input–output coefficients as variables rather than as constants. As relative prices change, factor proportions change, the degree of change being governed by the elasticity of substitution.[3]

To make this notion concrete, I would cite the present tendency of energy use and associated fuel inputs to decline per unit of output. This is happening on an overall scale because individual sectors and households are turning from relatively costly fuels to the use of energy-efficient capital and other ways of conserving BTUs. There is a time lag of adaptation and adjustment, but the laws of economics, especially the laws of production and consumption, are working, as they should, towards an eventual realization of full equilibrium.

Extensions of Supply Analysis

Supply side economics should not stop at the conventional boundaries, simply extending considerations of taxes, incentives or structural maladjustments. It should look at the subject from a wider perspective. I have already indicated how demography must be integrated more closely into the body of economic thought by

---

[3] See Preston, "The Wharton Long Term Model."

considering the age composition of the labor force, employment, and unemployment. I would go further and assert that demographic variables, on a broad basis, should be endogenous from the point of view of supply and demand side economics, but that is not actually the main thrust of the extension that I have in mind. It is only indicative.

Supply side issues that I have emphasized deal with the attaining of a good (non-inflationary) growth rate of GNP. That, in itself, is admirable, but should the GNP be our target variable? Economists are well aware of its failings to give a proper indication of economic welfare in some overall sense. If we were to reorient our theory of the functioning of the economy towards building a system that generates net economic welfare (NEW) instead of GNP, we would find that many supply side characteristics have to be introduced and emphasized. The quality, as well as the quantity, of conventionally measured goods and services would have to be taken into account. Many dimensions of the quality of life would have to supplement the GNP.

How is the GNP to be revised? We must include the costs of preserving the environment and of meeting some accepted standards of health and safety. Whether we have gone too far in regulation is not the matter to be decided. Once the degrees of regulation are accepted, then the positive values must be weighed against the negatives. That is part of the measurement calculus of the NEW, adding of the values of the bads and the goods, also including the non-market items.

Some of the directions that theoretical model-building must take in order to generate the NEW are evident. The pricing of capital goods should include enough to recoup the damage done to the environment by their operation. Housewives' inputs should be measured for the supply of labor by both themselves and their dependents.

In the pure case of by-product smoke pollution, the dimensions of the problem and analysis seem to be clear. In a conventional way of looking at things, let us assume that particulates that pollute the atmosphere are being produced together with good GNP. The overall package, however, is polluted, containing some bads together with the goods. If regulations are put into effect requiring additional cleaning equipment to be installed with ordinary production equipment, the cost of capital is increased, but the resulting GNP is of a high quality; it is clean. This is tantamount to raising the cost of capital to the investing enterprise and should produce opposite effects to lowering the cost of capital, say, as with an investment tax credit. We know from conventional model analysis that the investment tax credit leads to high output levels, with added investment. In the case of requiring clean-up equipment with conventional capital installations, we should correspondingly find less investment in conventional capital and less output. We would have less clean GNP after the introduction of the regulation than polluted GNP prior to the introduction of the regulation. Whether this is good or bad depends on how we value the *bads* in the polluted GNP and on how much clean GNP is left after the bads are subtracted.

If we were to realize that some inputs are used for environmental protection and some for the output of goods, we might not be so pessimistic about the trend of productivity, because some of the productive effort is being put to use to raise the NEW, although not necessarily the GNP. I do not believe that the GNP as presently measured is going to stand as the final goal.

This is more than redefinition of the problem; it is restructuring of our theoretical model. Keynesian economics blossomed after we had a vision of the equations that had particular values of GNP as their solution. Now the redirection of effort should be to develop equation systems that have NEW as their solution.

Appendix to Chapter 3

The most elementary principles of model-building to generate NEW may be outlined as follows. Let us consider a conventional model to generate GNP (J. R. Hicks's *IS–LM* specification).

$$S(r, Y) = I(r, Y)$$

$$M = L(r, Y)$$

where S = savings function
   I = investment function
   L = liquidity preference function
   r = interest rate
   Y = GNP
   M = money supply.

For simplicity, let us consider linear approximations to these two equations in order to derive some 'closed-form' expressions for the effects that interest us.

$$s_0 + s_r r + s_y Y = i_r r + i_y Y + i_0$$

$$M = l_r r + l_y Y + l_0$$

In the (r, Y)-coordinate plane, we have the two expressions

$$r = \frac{i_y - s_y}{s_r - i_r} Y + \frac{i_0 - s_0}{s_r - i_r}$$

$$\frac{i_y - s_y}{s_r - i_r} < 0, \frac{i_0 - s_0}{s_r - i_r} > 0$$

by usual stability assumptions;

$$r = \frac{l}{l_r} M - \frac{l_y}{l_r} Y - \frac{l_0}{l_r}$$

$$\frac{l_y}{l_r} < 0, \quad \frac{M - l_0}{l_r} > 0$$

by usual stability assumptions.

Graphically, we can depict the solution to this system given M, as in Figure 1.

Next, let us assume that investment in capital must allow for the purchase of anti-pollution devices, together with the GNP-creating capital goods. To make this example concrete, let us assume that $I(r, Y)$ is the decision function for purchase of capital such as generators for electric power, fueled by coal. The cost of acquiring and using this capital is indicated by r. It produces a "dirty" GNP, containing the smoke pollution of coal.

If the economy is regulated so that all generating equipment that burns coal must also provide for the simultaneous installation of stack scrubbers to keep the atmosphere clean, the cost of capital to the investor will rise from r to $r + \delta$. The saver will still realize just r; so the S and L functions are unchanged, but the I function is now written as

$$i_r(r + \delta) + i_y Y + i_0.$$

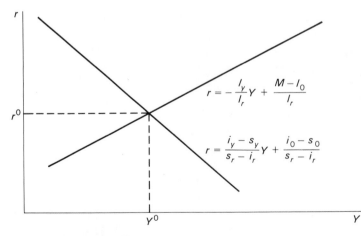

Figure 1   Solution for GNP

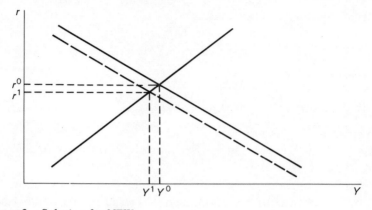

Figure 2   Solution for NEW

The equating of S and I now yields the relation

$$r = \frac{i_y - s_y}{s_r - i_r} Y + \frac{i_0 - s_0}{s_r - i_r} + \frac{i_r \delta}{s_r - i_r}.$$

The constant term is reduced by the absolute value of $i_r \delta / (s_r - i_r)$. The graphical solution is depicted in Figure 2.

The savings–investment equation shifts downwards, producing a solution with smaller values for both r and Y:

$$r^1 < r^0$$

$$Y^1 < Y^0.$$

In this highly simplified example, there is less NEW (in value terms) than GNP, because $Y^1 < Y^0$. But Y^1 is pollution-free (to an extent), while Y^0 is polluted. The issue is whether the public at large prefer clean Y^1 to dirty Y^0. This will depend on their preference function.

4 Supply Side Modeling

Demand Orientation

When there was an obvious shortfall of aggregate demand in the economy, US and worldwide, attention quite understandably centered on theoretical analysis that was oriented toward explanation of demand — its level, movement, and relationship to potential. Formal models to illustrate or develop them paid close attention to the components of demand and their summation, represented by GNP.

It is an overstatement to say that the models generated between the late 1930s and the 1960s looked only at the demand side of the economy. They all had aspects of general equilibrium analysis, in which a great deal of effort is devoted to discussion of the balance between supply and demand in the economy at large.

The demand emphasis comes from the practice of explaining GNP by first explaining its components and then forming, by addition, their total. The components consist of

family consumer expenditure
business fixed capital outlay
business inventory investment
residential construction
net exports
government spending on current and capital account.

Technically speaking, total demand is made up of the demand for component parts, but one of these parts represents demand for the purpose of further production. This is definitely true of business demand for fixed capital and partially true of residential construction and public capital formation. The goods demanded will be used in future production and thus will contribute to future supply. In fact, the present discussion of economic policy options focuses to a great extent on private capital formation for modernization and general enhancement of productivity, paving the way for better future supplies.

Consumer expenditures on education and training are similarly part of total demand (for services), but also represent investment in human capital. The aim for this kind of outlay is also for productivity enhancement.

Contemporary demand, therefore, has elements of supply, but it cannot be said that the typical demand-oriented model is also, automatically, a supply side model. The demand system elaborates, in great detail, the components of total demand. A demand-side model may go to great lengths to explain many kinds of durable, non-durable, and service expenditures – down to the details of gasoline and oil, furniture, clothing, food, rental housing, enter-tainment, and such refined categories. Similarly, many kinds of exports, imports, public outlays (federal, state, local), and business capital spending are given separate treatment. These items should be explained in both real and nominal terms, implying prices from ratios of the latter to the former.

The theoretical explanation of demand, both for components and for their total, is mainly academic. The complementary aspect of this analysis is the associated set of policy recommendations, under the heading of *demand management.* The thought here is that macro-policy formation can steer the economy by operation only at the overall level and not by interfering directly with the individual choice mechanism of conventional economic analysis. The control tools are

fiscal policy – public spending and taxing
monetary policy
commercial policy – foreign trade.

Public policy-makers are viewed as concentrating on these policies at the macro-level, "fine-tuning" the economy so that it performs just right – not too vigorously or too weakly.

The successes of these policies in bringing the main industrial economies of the world along a full employment path for two and a half decades after World War II are remarkable, but perhaps are underappreciated because of relatively poor economic performance during the 1970s. There is much dissatisfaction with policies of demand management at the present time and a groping for meaningful supply side policies. This prompts the present analysis of supply side model-building.

The policy apparatus of demand management is now spoken of, in pejorative terms, as Keynesian economics, and often is dismissed as having been the cause of present inflation with high-level unemployment that is so prevalent now in much of the world. Actually, Keynesian economic policy contributed much to the vigorous postwar expansion of the 1950s and 60s, and blocked a return to the depressed state of the world economy of the pre-World War II era, especially the 1930s. Both deliberate policy choices and the silent implementation of the automatic stabilizers were introduced in order to prevent a return to the depressed conditions of the 1920s and 30s. They function unnoticed whenever recessions or other economic adversity begin to prevail.

A new economic environment, from both the physical and the socio-political sides, and years of nearly full employment, to say nothing of the Vietnam War, led to the breakdown of the era of demand management. These policies cannot be dropped, but they cannot be relied upon to do the enormous job of steering the modern economy through overall policies alone.

In the next two sections, I shall try to outline the meaning of supply side components of the total economic model and the associated policy instruments. These are preludes to explicit statements of the new model that will judiciously try to accommodate both demand and supply components in one overall model of the system as a whole. It will not be a simple system, as many of the original demand models were. It will first search for what is needed in order to develop adequate analysis of the economy, and then consider whether the system can be simplified. There will be no premise that the final product will be as simple as the familiar multiplier–accelerator model, the *IS–LM* model, the monetarist model, or any other compact rendition.

The Meaning of the Supply Side

An abstract view of the economy is that it is made up of basic decision-making units – households and firms. At this point, an abstraction is being proposed, without regard to public sector units, financial sector units, or foreign units.

Households   Firms
demand goods = supply goods
supply factors = demand factors

Demand models focus attention on the demand for goods by households and the demand for factors by firms. The supply of factors by households and the supply of goods by firms are not treated in adequate detail. It is not that they are completely neglected; it is simply that they are not emphasized or displayed in detail.

Supply of Factors by Households

Labor supply is a principal activity of households and ultimately has an effect on unemployment, which is a key economic variable. Lying behind the relationships of labor supply, we find participation rates for various demographic groups and the whole issue of the demographic structure of the household sector.

Participation in the labor force, to be adequately handled, must be separately disaggregated by age, sex, and race. Possibly other groupings are relevant, too, but these are essential. Participation in these groupings must be based on the composition of the groupings. In other words, relationships to explain births, deaths, immigration, fertility, marriage, and health should be part of an adequate supply side model, unraveling back to demography. A great deal of demographic theory and institutions are significant in this respect, but the whole process makes more sense if there is a proper integration with economics of real wages, working hours, working conditions, and labor market conditions.

Labor supply will depend, among other things, on real wages. These will be net of taxes, but inclusive of transfers. Tax incentives must be properly included in economy-wide modeling, as has been done for some time. Proponents of tax reduction for its own sake argue on behalf of increasing incentives, but they are not aware of how much such incentives (or deterrents) are already taken into account for the construction of labor supply relationships. There may be some subjective impulses that are not adequately captured in present relationships, but there are very serious attempts already to reflect this aspect of economic behavior.

The other part of the supply side comes from the production of goods and services by firms. In demand-oriented models, factor demand, in the form of investment demand, is already accounted for. This is not an end in itself because capital goods are demanded in order to produce output on the supply side. Production functions or synthetic cost/supply functions are introduced for this purpose. A proper supply side model must go beyond the provision of aggregate production functions:

$$Y = F(K, L)$$

where Y = real value added output
  K = capital stock
  L = labor input.

It must go beyond the gross output function:

$$X = G(K, L, E, M)$$

where X = real value of gross output
  K = capital stock
  L = labor input
  E = energy input
  M = materials input.

Instead of basing the supply side model on just one or a few strict production functions of the *KLEM* type, it is better to introduce an entire input–output system to explain the supply side more carefully. The energy and materials (E and M) input values of the production function are taken directly from an input–output system. If they are both measured in constant dollar amounts for (approximate) use in the production function, they make up, together, the column sums of the input–output system.

When modeling the economy as a whole in highly aggregative fashion, we recognize that one sector's (intermediate) input is another sector's output. This is not true of the labor and capital inputs (L and K) as long as the input–output system refers entirely to intermediate flows and excludes capital flows. For the economy as a whole, therefore, it is sensible to use the value added version of the aggregate production function; for particular sectors, however, it is important to use the gross output function, because there may not be simple fixed or proportional relations between E and M on the one hand and X on the other.

An input–output system deals with the conceptual magnitudes such as X_{ij}, which represents the deliveries of intermediate goods and services from sector i to sector j. The production functions deal with E_j and M_j, the inputs of total energy and materials in sector j, regardless of where they came from.

The production functions are part of the standard macro-model of the economy as a whole, but disaggregated by sector. On an economy-wide basis, it is well known how to integrate this into a demand side model.[1] On a disaggregated sector basis, it is important to combine the input–output model with a macro-model of final demand, income generation, and market pricing. This system may be called the Keynes–Leontief system, named after the major figures in macroeconomics and inter-industry economics.

The formal structure of such a system is spelled out in detail in the Appendix. It has been implemented in the present version of the Wharton Annual Model and used for projections, scenario analysis, and economic policy analysis, usually over medium- (decade) and long-term (several decades) horizons. It is an interactive feedback system. The input–output system of inter-industry flows is driven by the final demand and income generation macro-models, but the latter cannot be solved without knowing the sectoral composition of output and pricing. The two systems must be solved together in joint dependency.

What are the features of this system that make it important for supply side modeling? This question will be answered under three headings:

 (i) Capacity constraints and "bottlenecks"
 (ii) Environment
(iii) Regulation.

---

[1] L. R. Klein, *The Keynesian Revolution* (New York: Macmillan, 1947), Appendix.

Capacity

If there is a shortfall in energy, food, or other resources, economic signals will be transmitted through prices or physical ceilings. The oil embargo of 1973–74 was a striking example of such a shortfall. A combination of the Wharton Annual Model, with the full input-output module, was used, together with the quarterly macro-model, to work out the immediate short-run cyclical consequences.[2] At that time, the Wharton Annual Model was ill equipped to deal with energy detail, but it has since been disaggregated into more energy sectors – coal, natural gas, oil, types of electric utilities, and types of fuel imports/exports.

Since energy is used in many intermediate processes, the input-output system showed where shortages of other products dependent on petroleum input would develop and where they, in turn, would limit the output of other products. Although energy use was a small fraction of total output (E/X), it had a large impact on the overall performance of the economy. This came about through its strategic role and the existence of bottlenecks. It was hard to put these ideas across in 1973–74, but they showed up clearly in input–output analysis.

After the physical limitations of the oil embargo of 1973–74, which caused an actual shortfall of some 2.0 million barrels per day, prices rose, not entirely as a result of market forces, but also through exercise of OPEC power. This caused relative prices to change drastically throughout the economy. They changed for other products besides fuels, and for a variety of reasons; nevertheless, it was important to have a modeling capability for indicating the effects of these changes on economic performance. This was done by introducing a new feature into input–output analysis – namely, to treat the technical coefficients as variables rather than parameters and to explain their shifts over time as functions of relative price changes. The use of the formulas

$$\frac{X_{ij}}{X_{Kj}} = \left(\frac{\alpha_{ij}}{\alpha_{Kj}}\right)^{\sigma_j}\left(\frac{P_i}{P_K}\right)^{-\sigma_j}$$

---

[2] L. R. Klein, "Supply Constraints in Demand Oriented Systems: An Interpretation of the Oil Crisis," *Zeitschrift für Nationalökonomie* 34 (1974): 45–56.

explained in the Appendix, show how relative input flows (into the jth sector) vary with relative price shifts according to the size of the elasticity of substitution, σ_j.

Environment

Concern with quality of air, water, solid waste, noise, traffic, and other congestion has intensified during recent years. Influence on the environment from these sources of disturbance is usually associated with particular lines of activity such as generation of electricity, production of steel, production of pulp/paper, chemical operations, and many others. A monitoring of the level of activity, by sector, in order to be able to estimate particulate waste products or other environmental hazards, is a first step. A large multi-sector model, like the Wharton Annual Model, enables us to generate sectoral output levels for this purpose. It is possible to build a separate model – a satellite model – showing the technical-engineering relationships that affect the environment, and using sectoral activity levels as inputs gives workable methods of auto-matically linking economic performance with environmental characteristics.

To protect the environment involves capital and operating costs. These would go into such devices as stack scrubbers for coal-fired electricity generation, filters for water purification, various disposal devices for waste products, muffling devices for noise, and other capital or operating systems for protecting the environment. These devices should be included in the costs of high-quality production – production that keeps the environment in better condition than would be achieved in their absence. The capital cost variables in the pricing and investment equations of the model should reflect the additional outlays that are needed for protection of the environment. Model scenarios or policy alterna-tives can be simulated with different degrees and mixtures of environmental measures inserted. They will have to be quantified, and, to the extent that they can be, the Keynes–Leontief system outlined in this paper is an excellent tool for studying their overall effects, including both direct and indirect influences.

Regulation

To a certain extent, protection of the environment is achieved through regulation of economic activity, but regulation is a much broader subject covering many more activities. Regulation of industry may be for occupational health/safety, for controlling rate of return on capital, for meeting efficiency standards, for allocating markets, or for promoting free competition. As in the case of environmental protection, regulation is often extremely worthy, but it is also often costly.

If regulation can be quantified, as in the case of environmental protection, it can be factored into the pricing decision. It may enter as a direct outlay for production or it may affect productivity. For example, the imposition of highway speed limits can be translated into an output slowdown for the trucking–transportation sector. Accident prevention and fuel efficiency must be taken into account on the plus side, while decreased productivity is allowed for on the other side. As productivity in the conventional sense falls, costs and price mark-up will rise. This kind of regulation will manifest itself in higher prices, reduced production, and lower demand. All these direct changes can be traced through the inter-industry sectors of an input–output system to get the full, indirect plus direct, effect.

Increasing attention is being paid to the economic cost of regulation and its contribution to inflation. The kind of model being discussed in this paper seems to be the way of getting at the issues. This is supply side modeling in every sense of the word.

Supply Side Policies

Macro-models and macro-policies of demand management developed together, hand-in-glove. Accordingly, supply side models and supply side policies fit together. Indeed, contemporary economic problems call forth new policies and these new policies need supply side models in order to interpret or understand their effects.

Supply side policies are different from macro-policies. The latter are not generally directed toward very specific economic activities or sectors of the economy. Supply side policies, by contrast, are sometimes called structural policies and are aimed at specific issues, specific economic activities, and specific groups.

One of the present ills of *stagflation* is the persistence of unemployment at levels above what we customarily recognize as full employment. Also, we have a maldistribution of unemployment; it is unduly concentrated among some groups in the economy, particularly young people. A structural policy would attempt to alleviate youth unemployment. It would make some contribution to overall unemployment through its impact on youth unemployment, but would be aimed specifically at reducing unemployment among a specific segment of the population. A macro-policy would simply try to reduce unemployment or increase employment all round, and, in doing so, might generate more inflationary pressure. A structural policy need not be inflationary. For example, one such policy is to lower the minimum wage, or possibly lower it separately for youths. In a model with well-defined labor supply, and demand relationships by demographic groups and minimum wages among the set of explanatory variables, it should be possible to analyze the potential benefits of changed legislation on minimum wages.

Similar structural policies concern changes in unemployment benefits (duration, amount, eligibility criteria) and social security contributions. It is conjectured that high unemployment benefits reduce incentives to find work and thereby to bring lower unemployment where possible, or that high social security contribution rates form a cost base on which prices are marked up, thus adding to inflationary pressures, particularly in these times of stagflation.

If the regulatory process is modeled in expanding the supply side information of a system, it is possible to examine structural policies of deregulation. It is not a matter of deregulating across the board, but of selective and gradual deregulation, not only to monitor the inflation content of the regulatory process, but also to study the impact of deregulation on economic performance in the affected branches of the economy.

Overall macro-policy on taxation might call for raising or lowering general tax rates on businesses and households in order to achieve GNP or other aggregative targets. A different kind of policy, on the supply side, might aim at adjusting tax rates or other tax parameters so as to stimulate capital formation. The main reason why that is attractive now is that higher levels of capital formation lead to improved productivity and eventually to a lessening of inflationary pressure. Thus, to get at the fundamentals of inflation from the supply side, it is desirable to encourage investment. Tax legislation on the form of investment credits, fast depreciation write-offs, credits for R & D, and favoritism for venture capital are all structural fiscal policies that are expected to work through the supply side. In the first instance, the effects may be most strongly felt on the demand side, but eventually they should show up on the supply side. An appropriate assessment of capital productivity in the *KLEM* production function will be strategic in judging the effect of such specific tax proposals.

Although the tax policies cited above are intended to work through the supply side, they were often proposed in the context of demand management in the early 1960s. Their supply effects are more important now. But they can be made more specific and more relevant for supply analysis by pinpointing them even more, toward such strategic sectors as energy investment, agricultural supply, or environmental protection. Differential credits favoring those kinds of capital formation that are most urgently needed are more structural, as policies, and more in the spirit of supply side analysis. Such fiscal changes are not intended to be varied cyclically. Their supply effects are long-term, and they should be maintained for long periods.

The principal structural policies that have been discussed are domestic, but many of the problems of the present US economy are international in nature — trade/payments deficits with dollar fluctuation. Highly structured commercial policies that seek to promote exports would seem to be called for in the present context. Better market research in foreign areas, higher efficiency in export industries, encouragement of potential new export industry lines, and more favorable financing terms for US exporters are all structural policies in the international trade sector that are wanting at the present time.

An Appropriate Role for Demand Models and Policies

The supply side model does not supplant the demand side; it only supplements it and rounds out the system so that both sides are modeled together. The same is true of economic policy. Macro-demand management policies have not been successful in dealing with many contemporary policies, but they did a great amount of good in other respects and continue to do so. They need structural and other supply side policies in order to meet a wider range of issues.

The Keynes–Leontief model outlined in equation form in the Appendix shows clearly that the total model requires the integration of relationships for aggregate demand and income generation together with supply side relations. The system is not decomposable and does not generally admit a solution to either the supply or demand sides separately. Both must be solved together.

In the case of policy formation, there must be full balance in measures to affect the main aggregates through overall fiscal spending, taxation, and monetary control. Policies directed along these lines cannot be expected to bring the economy into balanced equilibrium. There will still be rising prices and high unemployment in present circumstances. There will have to be policies to restrain energy consumption, enhance energy supplies, improve the distribution of unemployment, maintain agricultural output, encourage exports, and raise productivity.

5 Simulations of the Worldwide Impact of Oil Price Increases: an Exercise in Supply Side Economics

Background of Oil Price Analysis

According to the interpretations of supply side economics in this volume, an analytical study of resource limitations, leading to large increases in relative prices of a major scarce commodity – oil – is a typical example or application of this point of view. Since oil prices and oil trade – indeed, the functioning of the entire energy sector – have worldwide effects on both supplying (exporting) nations and demanding (importing) nations, this problem can best be understood in the context of a system of international trade flows. The econometric model of Project LINK is a well-known system for analyzing trade flows on a comprehensive basis.

The LINK model is an amalgamation of models from many countries and area groups covering the entire world. It presently includes models from 18 developed industrial countries (all members of OECD), eight centrally planned economy models, and four major regional models of the developing world – Latin America, Africa, the Middle East, and the Pacific Far East – with the possibility of a split among the OPEC and other developing countries. For the special long-run analysis examined in this chapter, it is necessary to refer back to a smaller earlier version of the present system, with only 13 industrial market economies and without the People's Republic of China in the centrally planned group.

Prepared by L. R. Klein with S. Fardoust, V. Filatov, and V. Su.

The LINK models have been described in greater detail elsewhere.[1] Briefly stated, they accept individual country or area models and combine these for simulation — forecasts, medium-term projections, policy analysis — in a way that forces some consistency of treatment. The integration of country or area models is implemented so that they produce a joint world economic solution that satisfies two important conditions:

World exports = world imports nominal, in current prices,
        by commodity group
World exports = world imports real, in constant prices,
        by commodity group

In order to force these two basic conditions to hold, we have to introduce conventions for a *numeraire* unit in world trade (US dollars). Valuation is f.o.b.

Standard International Trade Classification (SITC) categories conform to a lowest common denominator grouping across models. The interesting thing about this system for the problem at hand is that the structures of the models and their integration are such that separate country effects can be estimated, one by one, and their international repercussions with one another can also be estimated.

In the end, any country's or area's exports are weighted sums of partners' imports, the weights being rows of a world trade share matrix. Also, any country's or area's import prices are weighted sums of partners' export prices, the weights being columns of a world trade share matrix.

Fortunately, when the LINK system was first put together from a theoretical and logical viewpoint, there was a fundamental decision (in 1968) to treat the international trade flows of SITC 3 (mineral fuels) as one of the explicit commodity groups. This includes more than oil. It consists of several mineral fuels, but by examining each country or area, we can readily identify its exports and imports as coal, oil, gas, uranium, electricity, etc.

---

[1] R. J. Ball (ed.), *The International Linkage of National Economic Models* (Amsterdam: North Holland, 1973); J. Waelbroeck (ed.), *The Models of Project LINK* (Amsterdam: North Holland, 1976); J. Sawyer (ed.), *Modelling the International Transmission Mechanism* (Amsterdam: North Holland, 1979).

From the time of the oil embargo (November, 1973) and the large run-up in energy prices, it has been possible to detect some major changes in world economic prospects. Most major countries or areas outside the oil-exporting group expect to experience slower overall growth and more inflation than in the expansionary periods of recovery from World War II, which were featured by strong growth of world trade – the 1950s and 1960s. One indication of the degree of slowdown is given in my Nobel Lecture for 1980. Nominal interest rates are higher in the standard projection for the 1980s, as is the average unemployment rate, but the latter indicator could be lowered if the rate of growth in labor force slows down, as it apparently already has in the United States.

First, let us consider the downshifting in growth from a theoretical point of view. In a generalized version of the Harrod–Domar type of growth model, we estimate expansion of the economy from the scheme shown by the simple relationship:

$$sY = r(Y - Y_{-1})$$
$$\text{(Savings)} = \text{(Investment)}$$

The coefficient s is the savings ratio and r is the capital–output ratio. Y is real output. We assume that s and r depend on relative prices. As long as price ratios are steady, they can be treated as parameters.

$$Y = \frac{r}{r-s} Y_{-1}$$

$$Y_t = \left(\frac{r}{r-s}\right)^t Y_0.$$

If the capital–output ratio were 2.5 and the savings rate 0.1, we would have:

$$Y_t = (1.0417)^t Y_0.$$

The growth rate of the economy would be, for example, 4.17 percent. If the advent of something like the world energy "crisis" were to raise the relative price of energy to such an extent that more capital would be required to deal with this expensive input per unit of output, we would change the model to:

$$s(Y) = (r + \delta)(Y - Y_{-1})$$

$$Y_t = \left(\frac{r + \delta}{r + \delta - s}\right)^t Y_0$$

where δ stands for the view that the key ratios may depend on relative prices. If δ were as high as 0.5, the growth rate would fall from 4.17 percent to 3.45 percent, assuming that s is unaffected by this particular relative price change. In some lines of activity, the capital–output ratio in the United States did rise that much during the 1970s, but on average it rose more modestly – by about 0.08 during the first years after 1973 to about 0.02 by the end of the decade. Business investment, as a share of GNP, rose by about 1 percentage point. This figure, together with the rise in the estimated capital–output ratio, suggests that it became more difficult for the existing capital stock to produce an output flow; this is the fundamental reason for the slowdown in the growth rate, which is the same thing as saying that the incremental substitution of capital for energy produces less output than the incremental energy (it substituted for). Actually, the personal savings rate fell by about 3 percentage points during the 1970s. This, too, would make for a lower growth rate.

Once the capital stock is restructured to become more energy-efficient (efficiency → stock of capital produces same level of output at a lower energy input level), and people become more conservation minded, the capital–output ratio may fall back to its old levels, but as long as it remains elevated, there should be a tendency for growth to be slower than before. This slower growth may gradually fade with time adjustment and adaptation, but the national and international statistical models are estimating that it will prevail for the coming decade, when they assume that real energy prices will continue to rise. Also, the balance of payments disequilibrium and high import costs for energy induce restrictive monetary–fiscal policies in importing countries in order to deal with debt servicing and overall inflationary pressure. These factors contribute further to the general slowdown. Thus, the effect of the energy price rise (relatively) is to set back the volume of production in both level and rate of growth. This is the way it works out in practice and also according to the very simple growth model illustrated above.

Those parts of the world that are not disturbed by balance of payments deficits can continue to grow at a brisk pace, in many cases even faster. The oil-exporting nations are in this category. The oil-importing nations should, on balance, grow more slowly, although there will always be exceptional cases.

These are very general remarks that hold on average. The oil price shocks have differential impacts on the economies of oil-importing countries. In the United States, for example, consumer price has comparatively great sensitivity because energy-related consumption is a higher fraction of total consumption than in many other industrial countries. Also, the large amount of domestic energy production in the United States causes the GDP deflator to be quite sensitive to oil price shocks, where this would not be the case for countries that are even more dependent on imports. Apparently, Japan "learned" how to adjust to oil price shocks between 1973–74 and 1979–80. In the former case it was among the most sensitive, as measured by inflationary impact; in the latter case, it turned in an inflation report well below the OECD average.

As for the oil-exporting countries, they have differed according to the wisdom of investing their oil earnings in their own economies. Some have done much more than others by way of raising overall productivity and living standards. Long-range planning in some OPEC countries enabled them to enjoy a growth rate that was more insulated than in other countries against short-run changes in oil markets.

A Macro-model Explanation

The indicative examples of a simple growth model can show only what might happen to real stocks or flows, particularly production. The problem is more complex. It begins with a change in the pricing system and impacts on other markets, has effects on financial balance, and follows a more elaborate path throughout the economy. Figure 3 shows how oil prices work in the LINK system (see p. 58).

The higher prices set by OPEC appear as export prices in producing countries, particularly the developing countries. There is concentration in the Middle East, but Venezuela (Latin America), Indonesia (Pacific Far East), Nigeria (Africa), and a number of smaller countries have direct impact on other parts of the developing world. Also, Canada, the United Kingdom, and Norway are energy exporters among the OECD countries, as is the USSR in the centrally planned block.

The increased export prices, by virtue of the linking mechanism, show up as corresponding import price increases for purchasing countries. Within their country models this means a reduction in fuel imports (there is some small elasticity of demand; it varies among LINK OECD from -0.15 to -0.35). With lower fuel imports, capital use will be restrained; there will be greater unemployment (less employment) and a higher rate of inflation.[2]

Imports of goods and services will generally be reduced in the countries paying the higher prices for oil. This will occur in both fuel imports and overall imports, because the level of domestic activity will be reduced. It will also serve to increase export prices in the oil-importing countries because their costs will have gone up. Their imports will suffer and exports will also go down because export prices will rise. On balance, their net exports will fall.

As the oil-importing countries experience greater inflation and cut back on imports, this, by virtue of international linkage, will reduce exports of their partners and raise their partners' import prices further. These are the secondary, or international, repercussions.

All the effects together – the initial domestic effects on the oil-importing countries and their indirect impacts, through trade reductions, on partner countries – will lower world trade totals, raise world inflation rates, and lower world production activity. The secondary effects, which are by no means negligible, are the main feature of the linkage calculation. They occur after each

---

[2] See L. R. Klein, "The Longevity of Economic Theory," *Quantitative Wirtschaftsforschung*, ed. Horst Albach *et al.* (Tubingen: J. C. B. Mohr, 1977), 411–19, for an explanation and demonstration of the way that external price shocks manifest themselves in *more* inflation together with *more* unemployment.

importing country has started to absorb the initial domestic impacts and are transmitted around the world. This can be seen at the right side of Figure 3.

It is the purpose of the LINK system to work out the details of all the different effects, starting from the initial increases in oil prices, moving to domestic effects on importing countries, and then to the international transmission mechanism, looking back to the start of the process and continuing by iteration steps. Some of the reactions that make this system work are:

(i) monetary and fiscal intervention in the short-run by authorities to restrain inflation and deterioration of external accounts (these policies are implemented exogenously); conservation by households and firms who are sensitive to the high relative prices of energy or exogenous restrictions of energy use (short- to medium-run);

(ii) inter-fuel substitution as a result of relative price changes and substitution among major factor inputs (capital and labor substituted for energy) (medium- to long-run);

(iii) enhancement of energy supply as a result of relative price changes (long-run).

These effects are built into existing LINK models in various ways, each distinctive, for particular considerations in the separate countries. In the end, however, we find declines in energy use, as measured by the energy–GNP ratio, which has generally been falling since 1973. This is especially true of the United States.

Some Scenarios and System Sensitivities

Some of the key factors that make for differential impacts among countries are the ratio of energy to total consumption, energy production as a share of GNP, energy elasticities with respect to income and price, the OPEC recycling coefficient, wage indexing contracts, and exchange rate policy. The greater is the share of energy in total consumption, the greater will be the depressing effect of oil price rises on total consumption. The greater the OPEC recycling coefficients, the smaller the price impact, assuming that countries are not lulled into not making necessary adjustments

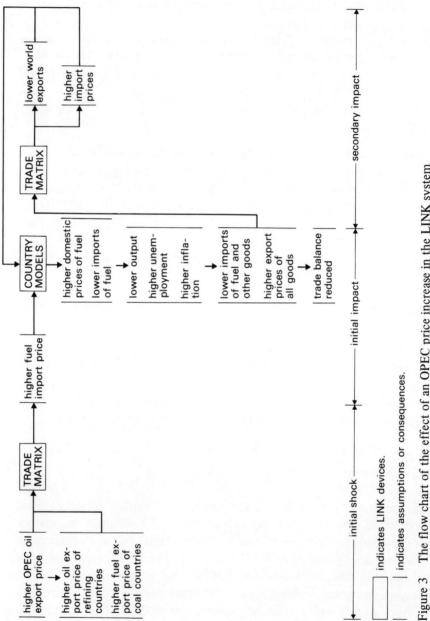

Figure 3   The flow chart of the effect of an OPEC price increase in the LINK system

in payment balances, as in the case of the United States, after the first oil shock. Income elasticity will be smaller, the smaller is the share of imports in total energy consumption. The larger the price elasticity, the smaller the impact on GDP and consumer price. Flexible exchange rates should enable a country to adapt more readily to changing energy prices. The fewer the number of rigid labor agreements on wages, indexing, and lay-offs, the more the economy can adjust through the labor market. By achieving a wage agreement at very moderate levels, Japan was able to come through the 1979–80 oil price shock relatively well, with low inflation rates and gains in real income for workers.

It may seem odd that a greater price elasticity will be associated with a smaller impact on GDP, because for a given price rise the direct effect will be for a larger decline in real demand as a consequence of the larger elasticity value. The second round effects are large enough to overcome the initial impact. If significant *conservation* is induced by the price rise, accompanied by a relatively larger elasticity, the payments balance of major importing countries will improve. This will hold up exchange rates, an anti-inflationary movement in itself, and will pose less of a barrier to fiscal or monetary stimulus to offset the oil shock. Rapidly falling oil imports and energy–GDP ratios take away the barriers to expansion and growth that come about in the second and additional rounds of the stretched-out recovery policy.

When the first major price rise occurred, in 1973–74, following the embargo on oil shipments, the importing world adjusted poorly, and industrial countries were thrown into a general recession, with high inflation rates. Some industrial countries followed a tight monetary and fiscal policy to lower the inflation impact, but this led to further decline in the level of economic activity. A more moderate policy would have led to higher output and employment levels. Oil exporters accumulated large surpluses which were soon eroded by virtue of dollar depreciation (the currency for oil prices), inflation in the industrial world which supplies manufactured exports to oil-rich nations, and their generally high marginal propensity to import.

After the second major price rise, 1979–80, the industrial world reacted more calmly. There was a spotty, non-synchronized slow-down, reaching recessionary dimensions in some places, but

Table 2 Gross national product, OECD (annual percentage change in real terms)

	1970	1971	1972	1973	1974	1975	1976	1977	1978	1979	1980
LINK OECD											
Australia	6.2	5.4	3.0	5.3	2.6	2.4	3.6	0.9	1.7	4.4	2.7
Austria	7.1	5.6	6.0	5.3	4.3	−1.7	5.8	4.4	1.0	5.1	3.6
Belgium	6.4	3.9	5.3	6.2	4.5	−1.9	5.3	0.8	3.0	2.4	1.4
Canada	2.6	7.0	5.8	7.5	3.4	1.1	5.8	2.4	3.6	2.9	0.1
Finland	7.9	1.8	7.5	6.5	3.2	0.6	0.3	0.4	2.3	7.2	5.3
France	5.7	5.4	5.9	5.4	3.2	0.2	5.2	2.8	3.6	3.2	1.3
Germany	6.0	3.2	3.7	4.9	0.5	−1.8	5.2	3.0	3.3	4.6	1.8
Italy	5.3	1.6	3.2	7.0	4.1	−3.6	5.9	1.9	2.6	5.0	4.0
Japan	9.8	4.6	8.8	8.8	−1.0	2.3	5.3	5.3	5.0	5.5	4.2
Netherlands	6.7	4.3	3.4	5.7	3.5	−1.0	5.3	2.4	2.5	2.2	0.8
Sweden	5.5	1.0	2.1	3.8	4.1	2.5	1.6	−2.4	1.4	4.0	1.4
United Kingdom	2.2	2.7	2.2	7.5	−1.2	−0.8	4.2	1.0	3.6	0.9	−1.8
United States	−0.1	2.9	5.8	5.4	−1.3	−1.0	5.6	5.1	4.4	2.4	−0.2
Other OECD Europe											
Denmark	2.6	2.4	5.4	5.2	−0.9	−0.6	7.9	1.8	1.3	3.5	−1.0
Greece	8.0	7.1	8.9	7.3	−3.6	6.1	6.4	3.4	6.2	3.8	0.6
Iceland	7.8	12.7	6.5	7.9	4.0	−0.5	3.5	5.8	5.2	2.6	2.5
Ireland	3.5	3.4	6.0	4.2	3.7	2.2	2.0	5.8	6.3	1.9	1.0
Luxemburg	1.6	4.1	5.9	10.2	4.7	−9.4	2.9	1.7	4.3	2.7	0.5
Norway	2.0	4.6	5.2	4.1	3.8	5.5	6.8	3.6	4.5	4.5	3.7
Portugal	9.1	6.6	8.0	11.2	1.1	−4.3	6.9	5.3	3.2	4.1	4.7
Spain	4.1	5.0	8.1	7.9	5.7	1.1	3.0	3.3	2.7	0.8	1.7
Total OECD less US	6.3	4.1	5.4	6.7	1.7	−0.3	5.1	2.9	3.5	3.7	2.1

Source: OECD Economic Outlook, July 1981.

Table 3 Consumer prices, OECD (annual percentage changes)

	1970	1971	1972	1973	1974	1975	1976	1977	1978	1979	1980
LINK OECD											
Australia	3.9	6.1	5.8	9.5	15.1	15.1	13.5	12.3	7.9	9.1	10.2
Austria	4.4	4.7	6.3	7.6	9.5	8.4	7.3	5.5	3.6	3.7	6.4
Belgium	3.9	4.3	5.5	7.0	12.7	12.8	9.2	7.1	4.5	4.5	6.6
Canada	3.3	2.9	4.8	7.6	10.8	10.8	7.5	8.0	9.0	9.1	10.1
Finland	2.8	6.5	7.1	10.7	16.9	17.9	14.4	12.2	7.8	7.5	11.6
France	5.2	5.5	6.2	7.3	13.7	11.8	9.6	9.4	9.1	10.8	13.6
Germany	3.4	5.3	5.5	6.9	7.0	6.0	4.5	3.7	2.7	4.1	5.5
Italy	5.0	4.8	5.7	10.8	19.1	17.0	16.8	18.4	12.1	14.8	21.2
Japan	7.7	6.1	4.5	11.7	24.5	11.8	9.3	8.1	3.8	3.6	8.0
Netherlands	3.6	7.5	7.8	8.0	9.6	10.2	8.8	6.4	4.1	4.2	6.5
Sweden	7.0	7.4	6.0	6.7	9.9	9.8	10.3	11.4	10.0	7.2	13.7
United Kingdom	6.4	9.4	7.1	9.2	16.0	24.2	16.5	15.8	8.3	13.4	18.0
United States	5.9	4.3	3.3	6.2	11.0	9.1	5.8	6.5	7.7	11.3	13.5
Other OECD Europe											
Denmark	5.8	5.8	6.6	9.3	15.3	9.6	9.0	11.1	10.0	9.6	12.3
Greece	3.2	3.0	4.3	15.5	26.9	13.4	13.3	12.1	12.6	19.0	24.9
Iceland	13.6	6.6	9.7	20.6	42.9	49.1	33.0	29.9	44.9	44.1	57.5
Ireland	8.2	8.9	8.7	11.4	17.0	20.9	18.0	13.6	7.6	13.3	18.2
Luxemburg	4.6	4.7	5.2	6.1	9.5	10.7	9.8	6.7	3.1	4.5	6.3
Norway	10.6	6.2	7.2	7.5	9.4	11.7	9.1	9.1	8.1	4.8	10.9
Portugal	6.3	8.3	8.9	11.5	29.2	20.4	19.3	27.2	22.5	23.9	16.6
Spain	5.7	8.3	8.3	11.4	15.7	16.9	17.7	24.5	19.8	15.7	15.5
Total OECD	5.6	5.3	4.7	7.8	13.5	11.3	8.6	8.9	7.9	9.8	12.9

Source: OECD Economic Outlook, July 1981.

Table 4 OPEC current balance (US$billions)

	1973	1974	1975	1976	1977	1978	1979	1980
Trade balance	21.5	77.0	49.5	65.0	61.5	42.5	114.0	169.0
Current balance	7.7	59.5	27.2	36.5	29.0	4.5	66.0	121.0

Source: OECD Economic Outlook, December 1980 and July 1981.

not in the form of a world business cycle. Inflation flared up again, but not on the scale that occurred after 1974.

These movements are apparent in Tables 2–7. The reader should pay particular attention to the tables as follows.

Table 2: The concentration of negative entries for 1975 and also in 1974: this resulted in an overall negative value for the average growth rate. There was a slow-down in 1980 (in 1979, too, for the United States), but with fewer negatives and a higher average than in 1975.

Table 3: A large increase in inflation rates, starting in 1973 and continuing until 1975, at least. Another flare-up in inflation is apparent in 1979–80. These results show up clearly in the average figures.

Table 4: The OPEC surplus had practically been reduced to zero by 1978. It rises again by 1979–80.

Table 5: The exchange rate movements of capital surplus OPEC members (Kuwait, Libya, Qatar, Saudi Arabia, and United Arab Emirates) bears very little relationship to the amount of current balance surplus they accumulated each year. This is because the governments of these countries (which have a monopoly for the production and export of oil) do not have to inject all their oil income in local currency into the domestic economies. Therefore, the demand for oil exports bears little relation to demand for local currencies of these exporters. While the OECD currencies move against one another according to the size of current account deficits (or surpluses) among other factors, OPEC's currencies are rigidly tied to the OECD currencies (for example, SDR). This is true regardless of the size of surplus. Therefore, the traditional adjustment

Table 5 Exchange rate and current balances of capital surplus OPEC members and the major seven industrial countries

	1973	1974	1975	1976	1977	1978	1979	1980	1973-80 (compound average)
OPEC (capital surplus members)	National currency units per US dollar (annual percentage change)								
Kuwait	+9.4	+2.3	-1.5	+2.4	+2.3	+2.9	-0.5	0.0	+1.9
Libya	+10.0	0.0	0.0	0.0	0.0	0.0	0.0	0.0	+1.2
Qatar	+10.0	0.0	-1.0	+0.7	+0.0	+3.0	+3.4	+1.7	+1.9
Saudi Arabia	+14.4	0.0	+0.5	0.0	+0.7	+5.4	-1.5	+1.2	+2.3
United Arab Emirates	+8.6	+1.4	+0.0	-0.4	+0.5	+1.9	+1.8	+2.5	+1.9
Current account of OPEC's "low absorbers" (US$billions)	7.0	35.5	25.2	29.2	27.5	15.5	44.0	101.0	
	US dollar per SDR (annual percentage change)								
United States ($/SDR)	-11.1	-1.5	+4.3	+0.7	-4.5	-7.2	-1.1	+3.1	
US current balance (US$billions)	7.1	4.8	18.2	4.3	-14.0	-14.2	-0.7	+0.1	
Major six industrial[a] countries, current balance (US$billions)	-1.3	-17.8	-5.8	-7.2	5.6	13.8	-15.3	-39.3	

[a] Japan, France, Italy, Germany, United Kingdom, and Canada.

Table 6 Effect of exchange rate changes upon import price of oil (from OPEC) by major importing countries, 1973–81 (annual percentage changes)

Years	Annual % change in nominal oil prices (OPEC) in US dollars	Japan A	Japan B	Germany A	Germany B	France A	France B	Italy A	Italy B
1973	26.8	−12.0	14.8	−16.3	10.5	−11.7	15.1	0.0	26.8
1974	287.4	+7.7	295.1	−2.9	284.5	+8.1	295.5	+11.6	299.0
1975	0.7	+1.7	2.4	−5.0	−4.3	−10.8	−10.1	0.0	0.7
1976	8.1	0.0	8.1	+2.4	10.5	+11.4	19.5	+27.4	35.5
1977	9.6	−9.7	−0.1	−7.9	1.7	+2.7	12.3	+6.0	15.6
1978	0.5	−21.6	−21.1	−13.3	−12.8	−8.1	−7.6	−4.7	−4.2
1979	40.8	+4.3	45.1	−18.9	31.9	−5.7	35.1	−2.1	38.7
1980	68.2	+3.5	71.7	−0.7	67.5	−0.5	67.7	+3.0	71.2
1981[a]	20.0	−5.2	14.8	+21.6	41.6	+37.2	57.2	+27.3	47.3
Compound average	32.3	−3.0	29.3	−3.1	29.2	+1.6	33.9	+7.2	39.5

[a] LINK estimate.
A Percentage change in local currency price of US dollar.
B Effective percentage change in nominal price of oil imported from OPEC (f.o.b.).

Table 7 Estimated disposition of OPEC surplus, 1974-80 (US$billions)

	1974	1975	1976	1977	1978	1979*	1980*
Percentage of total OPEC reserves held in dollars (%)	73.0	84.0	95.0	97.0	93.0	N.A.	N.A.
(a) Surplus current balance	60.0	28.0	37.0	30.0	5.0	68.0	116.0
Disposition of OPEC's investable surplus (US$billions)							
United States	13.0	9.5	12.0	9.3	1.8	7.1	14.2
Eurodollar market	23.0	8.0	11.0	12.0	2.5	14.8[a]	14.8[a]
United Kingdom	7.5	0.3	−1.0	0.75	−0.3	2.4	2.8
Other developed countries	6.0	7.8	8.0	8.0	6.0	27.4	42.9[b]
Developing countries	6.0	7.3	7.5	8.5	4.3	9.6	6.6
Eastern Europe and USSR	0.5	2.0	1.3	1.3	0.5	N.A.	N.A.
International financial organizations	3.8	4.3	1.8	0.5	−0.5	−0.4	4.9
(b) Total	59.8	39.2	40.6	40.4	14.3	61.0	86.2
(c) OPEC's gross borrowings	0.5	4.0	8.0	10.0	15.0	N.A.	N.A.
(d) Statistical discrepancy or unidentified dispositions (a + c − b)	0.7	−7.2	4.4	−0.4	+5.7	+8.0	+29.8

Combined figures (United Kingdom + Other developed countries): 1974 = 13.5; 1975 = 8.1; 1976 = 7.0; 1977 = 8.8; 1978 = 5.7; 1979* = 29.8; 1980* = 45.7.

* Rough estimates derived from various sources
[a] 1979 and 1980 figures only include Eurocurrency bank deposits in UK.
[b] 1979 and 1980 figures include investments and bank deposits.
Source: US Treasury Bulletins; Office of International Banking and Portfolio; *Bank of England Quarterly Bulletins.*

mechanisms are not allowed to work in this case. Furthermore, the current balance statistics underestimate the size of the surplus since they do not account for the investments of the oil producers in any given period.

Table 6: Changes in exchange rates of the major oil importers *vis-à-vis* the US dollar have an important effect on the size of the actual impact of the oil price increases on the domestic economy. For example, in 1978, when oil prices were stable, Japan, Germany, France, and Italy were all facing falling oil prices because their currencies appreciated against the dollar. The situation is different in 1981 because major European currencies have depreciated sharply against the dollar.

Table 7: The distribution of OPEC's surplus among different OECD countries and their currency denominations are important in determining the changes in exchange rates among the OECD countries. Up to now most of OPEC's reserves and investments have been in US dollars.

Simulations of the LINK System

We have simulated the LINK system under two sets of conditions:

(i) a baseline case, in which the world oil price is assumed to grow at world inflation (zero real growth) defined by the rate of growth of OECD export prices (about 6.5 percent);

(ii) an oil price shock case, in which the oil export price is raised by 10 percent for four years (1982–85) over the base case. Export prices of other fuels are incremented by one-half as much.

The overall impact in 13 LINK OECD countries, in the aggregate, is shown in Table 8b.[3] The simulation suggests that the average annual world growth rate of GDP would decline by 0.4 to 0.5 percentage points between 1982 and 1985 if the real oil price were to rise by about 10 percent per year. This observed pattern for real-world GDP is evident for the volume of real-world exports

---

[3] The 13 LINK OECD countries are Australia, Austria, Belgium, Canada, Finland, France, Germany, Italy, Japan, Netherlands, Sweden, United Kingdom, and United States.

as well. The growth rate of real-world trade falls by 0.3 and 0.5 percent in 1982 and 1983 with the growth rate trend reversing in 1985. The incidence varied yearly, and the delayed pattern reversal indicates that the future effects of a one-time real price increase are moderate and of the opposite sign, offsetting future real price increases as world trade recovers from the earlier shocks.

The world inflation rate is estimated to increase by about 0.9 percent, and this effect is a persistent one with no signs of reversal.

The effects on the industrial market economies is somewhat different (Table 8b). A 9–10 percent rise in the real-world oil price would reduce industrial countries' growth by one-half, but the trade volume effect is larger. The industrial countries' growth

Table 8a Effects of a sustained 10 percent increase in the world oil price, 1982-85 (deviation of growth rates from the base case)

	1982	1983	1984	1985
1 Real exports of goods	−0.3	−0.5	−0.4	0.2
2 Export price of goods	2.1	2.4	2.4	2.3
3 GDP (1970 $ and exchange rates)[a]	−0.4	−0.5	−0.5	−0.4
4 Price deflator GDP[b]	0.7	0.9	0.9	0.9
5 Real exports of goods in SITC 3	−0.4	−0.5	−0.4	−0.2

[a] World = 0.6565 * OECD + 0.1494 * DEVE + 0.1851 * CMEA.
  DEVE = Developing.
[b] World = 0.8145 * OECD + 0.1855 * DEVE. Comprehensive inflation measures for CMEA are not available.

Table 8b Effects of a sustained 10 percent increase in the world oil price, 1982-85, LINK OECD countries, industrial market economies (deviation of growth rates from the base case)

	1982	1983	1984	1985
1 Real exports of goods	−0.8	−1.0	−1.0	−0.4
2 Real imports of goods	−0.6	−1.0	−0.8	−0.1
3 GDP (1970 $ and exchange rates)	−0.4	−0.5	−0.5	−0.4
4 Price deflator, GDP	+ 0.1	+ 0.2	+ 0.2	+ 0.0
5 Price deflator, consumer expenditures	+ 0.5	+ 0.6	+ 0.7	+ 0.5

path is lowered to this new medium-term path after one year. The main losers are Japan and Australia, with North America in second place. The average real GDP growth rate decline is more than 0.5 percent in both regions. Western Europe seems to adapt better, suffering only a 0.2 percent cutback in its aggregate GDP growth rate.

The GDP decline in industrial countries is accompanied by a corresponding decline in the non-oil-exporting developing countries that varies between 0.6 and 1.0 percent per annum. This drop steadily changes, reaching 1.0 percent in 1985.

Inflation variability also prevails across the OECD regions. For the industrial countries as a whole, a 10 percent real oil price hike raises consumer price inflation by a bit more than one-half percentage point. The North American and Western European inflation rates rise by slightly more than one-half percentage point in the 1982–85 period, while Japan's inflation rate rises by only about 0.3 percent. Although both North America and Japan have similar GDP growth rate reactions, North America's inflation response is twice that of Japan's. As pointed out earlier, apparently, Japan "learned" how to adjust to oil price shocks in the crisis periods of the 1970s.

The developing country models in LINK provide more meaningful estimates of overall GDP prices than of other prices: therefore, in Table 8a the inflation rate, which jumps by almost one whole percentage point, is measured by this overall statistic.

It should be noted that for the industrial countries in Table 8b the inflationary impact is more pronounced in consumer prices than in the GDP deflator. This is because the full effect of imports is retained in consumer expenditures, which may be outlays for either imported or domestic goods. The GDP, on the other hand, has only indirect import content; it is the production of goods by domestic sources. It should be re-emphasized that the effect on trade volume is larger than the effect on production. The 1960s was a period of rapid trade expansion, accompanying a strong growth rate of production. In the 1980s we look for more modest trade expansion to accompany output growth, which, in turn, is expected to be somewhat smaller. These sensitivity calculations indicate why we generally project less growth and more inflation than along the baseline path during the 1980s.

Table 9 summarizes the sensitivity of the LINK system to oil price shocks in comparison with results from the OECD INTER-LINK model. The results are for OECD (LINK 13 in our case) and selected industrial countries.

Two possible price paths for oil exports over the whole decade of the 1980s are:

(a) indexing of oil prices to OECD export prices (measured in US dollars). This is implemented with a lag of one year. It is close to case (i) above, but not identical. In 1981 and 1982 the price is set higher — 12.5 and 11.5 percent growth, respectively;[4]

(b) indexing of oil prices to the same OECD export price as in (a) and also to OECD real output growth. Scenario (a) has a real price increase of a fraction of a percent annually, while (b) has a real price increase of 3.0–4.0 percent annually. Scenario (b) is close to the OPEC "formula" for oil pricing. This is not an officially adopted formula, but has presumably been discussed in OPEC gatherings.

Year-by-year and quinquennium or decade growth rates are given in the summary Tables 10a and 10b. Some more regional and country details are also given. By comparing Tables 10a and 10c with 10b and 10d, we can see that growth is reduced by the higher of the two price formulas, with greater effect coming in the second half of the decade, but there is an estimated drop of 0.2 percentage points in OECD growth as early as 1982. The inflation rate is higher in scenario (b) than (a), and the effect is somewhat more pronounced in the second half of the decade. The oil-importing developing countries are hit significantly by the shift

---

[4] It may appear to be strange that these price increases are set for a period, 1981–82, when it is accepted that there is an "oil glut" with falling spot prices. In some cases, contract prices have also been reduced. As for 1981, much of the increase occurred already, prior to the full recognition of the glut, and the arithmetic of year-to-year comparisons shows that the increase of 12.5 percent is quite plausible. The glut is temporary and can be greatly affected by the oil-exporting countries in OPEC. The price increase of 11.5 percent for 1982 is greater than the actual change, which is slightly negative, but the figure used is consistent with the OPEC indexing formula, being only slightly in excess of the formula value. Troubled events in the Middle East suggest that the glut and falling spot prices may be only a temporary energy situation, and we could well see firming trends soon. This indicates why the two increments for 1981–82 are easier to accept than projections based on no change in prices or even on declines in an oversold market.

Table 9 Sensitivity of the OECD and LINK econometric
models to oil price changes (deviations of growth
rates from baseline)

Oil prices (nominal)	OECD[a] 10%	LINK 10%
OECD		
GDP	−0.3	−0.4
Exports	−0.2	−0.8
Imports	−0.7	−0.6
PC (consumption deflator)	+ 0.7	+ 0.5
GDP		
United States	−0.3	−0.6
Germany	−0.2	−0.2
France	−0.2	−0.3
United Kingdom	−0.0	−0.2
Canada	−0.0	+ 0.3
Japan	—	—
PC		
United States	+ 0.6	+ 0.6
Germany	+ 0.7	+ 0.0
France	+ 0.6	+ 1.2
United Kingdom	+ 0.5	+ 0.7
Canada	+ 0.2	+ 0.5
Japan	—	—

[a] OECD's INTER-LINK model.

to a formula with higher prices. The centrally planned economies
appear to have a much better trade balance in scenario (b), but
growth rates differ only slightly. The oil-exporting countries
maintain a strong trade surplus throughout scenario (b), but fall
approximately to balance (zero) in scenario (a).

Table 11 presents the summary results of LINK system and
FUGI Global Macroeconomic Model of Soka University, Japan,
for similar indexation exercises. Although, the two systems are
quite different in their structures and emphasis, in some cases
they have strikingly similar elasticities.

During the 1970s, there were two disturbances that set off
steps in the time curve of oil prices. The first disturbance was the
October war in the Middle East in 1973, and the second was the
Iranian revolution in 1979. The first step in oil prices caused, as

we noticed earlier, a synchronized world recession; the second caused mixed cyclical responses. The main reason for the synchronized decline in 1973–74 is that many major countries were already in the midst of slowdowns generated by restrictive monetary, fiscal, and other policies to deal with the inflationary buildup of 1973. When restricted oil imports became a reality for several countries at once, when they were engaged in a deliberate policy of restraining their overall economies, it becomes clear that the oil shock was readily translated into a synchronized recession. In the second round of oil price rises, following the Iranian revolution of 1979, there were no such policies of restraint in force on a broad scale. Also, many countries, including the United States, were learning to adjust to new life styles and production conditions in an era of expensive energy. The energy–GDP ratio had declined substantially since 1973 and was still falling in many large countries. In this situation, a synchronized recession did not develop.

It is of some interest to simulate a similar disturbance and step in oil prices during the decade of the 1980s. We have accordingly introduced an 80 percent price rise for 1986, as an example of a disturbance during this decade. This could be induced by a major event or simply by a lack of balance between world demand and world supply coming to a supply shortage by 1986, assuming that price was growing on a path of about 7 percent up to that time.

The baseline case for comparison with this shock scenario is a nominal rise of 10 percent annually in oil prices, after a transitional value of 25 percent in 1981, coming down from the large increments of 1979 and 1980.[5] In the shock case, we assume that prices follow a path of practically zero real price change during 1982–85. The two assumptions are shown in Table 12.

This kind of mid-decade disturbance is much like the pattern of the first oil shock. The large rise came in 1974–75, and real prices fell after that period, but nominal prices held firm or increased. The final price reached in 1980 is practically identical in both cases, as shown by the bottom line in Table 12.

---

[5] Since the development of an oil glut in 1981, spot prices have fallen and the yearly average increase for 1981 will work out to be less than 25 percent – more like 12 percent. For *comparative* simulation purposes, though, this high value for 1981 is not important as such. What matters is the estimated difference between two scenarios.

Table 10a Project LINK world summary of measures of growth and inflation: oil prices indexed to OECD export prices (annual percentage changes)[a]

Country grouping	1980	1981	1982	1983	1984	1985	1986	1987	1988	1989	1990	1980–85g	1985–90g	1980–90g
Gross domestic product														
13 LINK OECD countries[b]	1.3	2.6	4.6	4.1	3.7	3.1	3.2	3.1	3.7	4.3	3.9	3.6	3.6	3.6
Level[c]	2613.5	2681.8	2804.6	2917.8	3026.0	3120.2	3218.1	3317.9	3439.6	3584.6	3724.3			
US and Canada	−0.7	2.9	5.0	4.4	3.5	2.5	2.8	2.9	3.9	4.9	4.3	3.7	3.8	3.7
Japan and Australia	4.6	3.8	4.8	4.6	4.6	4.5	3.7	3.4	3.6	3.5	3.5	4.5	3.5	4.0
Rest of OECD	3.0	1.6	3.6	3.2	3.8	3.6	3.6	3.4	3.4	3.5	3.3	3.1	3.4	3.3
Developing countries	5.0	5.1	5.1	5.4	5.4	5.5	5.7	5.6	5.8	6.0	6.1	5.3	5.8	5.6
Non-oil exporting	5.5	5.1	5.1	5.4	5.4	5.6	5.6	5.5	5.7	5.9	6.1	5.3	5.8	5.5
Oil exporting	2.2	5.3	5.3	5.3	5.3	5.3	6.3	6.3	6.3	6.3	6.3	5.3	6.3	5.8
Centrally planned countries[d]	4.2	3.4	4.2	4.4	4.6	4.4	4.4	4.6	4.4	4.7	4.6	4.2	4.5	4.4
World[e]	2.0	3.1	4.6	4.3	4.1	3.7	3.7	3.7	4.1	4.5	4.3	3.9	4.1	4.0

Private consumption
deflator

13 LINK OECD													
countries	11.4	8.0	6.5	5.8	5.7	5.5	5.4	5.2	4.8	4.2	4.1	6.3	4.7	5.5
(GDP deflator)	9.5	7.9	6.5	5.9	5.9	5.7	5.7	5.4	5.2	4.5	4.3	6.4	5.0	5.7
US and Canada	10.4	7.9	6.2	5.4	5.7	5.4	5.4	5.0	4.5	3.3	3.3	6.1	4.3	5.2
Japan and Australia	6.9	8.1	6.9	6.1	5.6	5.7	5.6	5.3	5.4	5.3	5.2	6.5	5.4	5.9
Rest of OECD	14.6	8.0	6.7	6.4	5.7	5.7	5.4	5.3	5.3	5.1	4.9	6.5	5.2	5.9
Developing countries	33.9	27.5	20.2	17.7	14.9	12.0	9.4	8.9	8.2	7.4	6.7	18.4	8.1	13.1
Non-oil exporting	36.8	28.9	21.9	19.1	16.1	12.7	9.9	9.4	8.6	7.8	7.1	19.6	8.5	13.9
Oil exporting	13.5	17.9	8.5	7.9	7.1	6.9	5.8	5.6	5.1	4.5	4.0	9.6	5.0	7.3
World[f]	15.6	11.6	9.0	8.0	7.4	6.7	6.1	5.9	5.5	4.8	4.6	8.5	5.4	6.9

[a] Weighted averages of own country/region growth rates.

[b] Thirteen LINK OECD countries are: Australia, Austria, Belgium, Canada, Finland, France, Federal Republic of Germany, Italy, Japan, Netherlands, Sweden, United Kingdom and the United States of America.

[c] Billions of 1970 US $ at 1970 exchange rates.

[d] Includes only Eastern Europe CMEA and the USSR.

[e] World = 0.6565 * OECD + 0.1494 * DEVE + 0.1851 * CMEA.

[f] World = 0.8145 * OECD + 0.1855 * DEVE. Inflation measures for CMEA are not available.

[g] Period averages are calculated as the geometric mean of the second through last period growth rates.

Table 10b Project LINK world summary of measures of growth and inflation: oil prices indexed to OECD export prices and OECD real output growth (annual percentage changes)[a]

Country grouping	1980	1981	1982	1983	1984	1985	1986	1987	1988	1989	1990	1980–85[g]	1985–90[g]	1980–90[g]
Gross domestic product														
13 LINK OECD														
countries[b]	1.3	2.6	4.4	3.9	3.7	3.2	3.1	3.0	3.3	3.5	3.2	3.6	3.2	3.4
Level[c]	2613.5	2679.7	2797.5	2905.7	3013.5	3109.3	3205.9	3302.1	3410.5	3527.5	3641.5			
US and Canada	−0.7	2.8	4.8	4.2	3.6	2.7	3.4	2.9	3.3	3.7	3.3	3.6	3.2	3.4
Japan and Australia	4.6	3.7	4.7	4.4	4.3	4.3	3.4	3.1	3.3	3.1	3.2	4.3	3.2	3.7
Rest of OECD	3.0	1.6	3.5	3.0	3.7	3.5	3.5	3.2	3.3	3.3	3.2	3.1	3.3	3.2
Developing countries	5.0	5.0	4.9	5.1	5.1	5.2	5.3	5.2	5.3	5.4	5.6	5.1	5.4	5.2
Non-oil exporting	5.5	5.0	4.9	5.1	5.0	5.2	5.2	5.1	5.2	5.2	5.5	5.0	5.2	5.1
Oil exporting	2.2	5.3	5.3	5.3	5.3	5.3	6.3	6.3	6.3	6.3	6.3	5.3	6.3	5.8
Centrally planned														
countries[d]	4.2	3.4	4.2	4.4	4.6	4.4	4.4	4.6	4.5	4.7	4.6	4.2	4.6	4.4
World[e]	2.0	3.1	4.4	4.1	4.1	3.7	3.7	3.6	3.8	3.9	3.8	3.9	3.8	3.8

Private consumption
deflator

13 LINK OECD countries	11.4	8.1	6.7	6.1	5.8	5.7	5.5	5.5	5.4	5.0	4.8	6.5	5.2	5.8
(GDP deflator)	9.5	7.9	6.6	6.0	5.7	5.7	5.5	5.6	5.5	5.0	4.7	6.4	5.3	5.8
US and Canada	10.4	8.1	6.4	5.7	5.6	5.5	5.3	5.4	5.2	4.5	4.2	6.2	4.9	5.6
Japan and Australia	6.9	8.2	7.0	6.3	5.8	5.8	5.7	5.5	5.5	5.4	5.3	6.6	5.5	6.0
Rest of OECD	14.6	8.1	7.0	6.7	6.0	6.0	5.7	5.7	5.7	5.6	5.5	6.8	5.7	6.2
Developing countries	33.9	27.9	22.1	18.6	15.8	12.7	10.3	9.9	9.4	9.0	8.2	19.1	9.4	14.1
Non-oil exporting	36.8	29.3	22.8	20.1	17.0	13.5	10.9	10.5	10.0	9.5	8.7	20.4	9.9	15.1
Oil exporting	13.5	18.0	8.8	8.2	7.4	7.2	6.2	6.0	5.8	5.5	4.9	9.9	5.7	7.8
World[f]	15.6	11.8	9.4	8.4	7.6	7.0	6.4	6.3	6.1	5.7	5.4	8.8	6.0	7.4

a Weighted averages of own country/region growth rates.

b Thirteen LINK OECD countries are: Australia, Austria, Belgium, Canada, Finland, France, Federal Republic of Germany, Italy, Japan, Netherlands, Sweden, United Kingdom and the United States of America.

c Billions of 1970 US $ at 1970 exchange rates.

d Includes only Eastern Europe CMEA and the USSR.

e World = 0.6565 * OECD + 0.1494 * DEVE + 0.1851 * CMEA.

f World = 0.8145 * OECD + 0.1855 * DEVE. Inflation measures for CMEA are not available.

g Period averages are calculated as the geometric mean of the second through last period growth rates.

Table 10c Project LINK world trade summary: oil prices indexed to OECD export prices (US$billions)[a]

	1980	1981	% Change	1982	% Change	1983	% Change	1984	% Change	1985	% Change	1986	% Change
13 LINK OECD countries[b]													
Exports[c]	1036.0	1218.4	17.6	1437.3	18.0	1616.9	12.5	1821.7	12.7	2046.5	12.3	2298.3	12.3
Imports	1090.0	1242.5	14.0	1414.2	13.8	1590.9	12.5	1791.4	12.6	1994.0	11.3	2210.5	10.9
Balance	−54.0	−24.1		23.0		26.1		30.2		52.5		87.9	
US and Canada													
Exports[c]	268.5	305.6	13.8	373.7	22.3	426.9	14.2	475.1	11.3	526.2	10.7	588.9	11.9
Imports	293.2	332.3	13.3	380.6	14.5	431.4	13.3	482.6	11.9	529.8	9.8	579.9	9.9
Balance	−24.7	−26.8		−7.0		−4.5		−7.5		−3.6		9.0	
Japan and Australia													
Exports[c]	138.1	157.1	13.8	200.1	27.3	234.5	17.2	271.0	15.6	315.2	16.3	348.9	10.7
Imports	139.6	155.3	11.3	178.0	14.6	203.4	14.3	228.6	12.4	255.2	11.6	279.6	9.6
Balance	−1.5	1.8		22.1		31.1		42.4		60.1		69.3	
Rest of OECD													
Exports[c]	629.4	755.7	20.1	863.6	14.3	955.5	10.7	1075.6	12.6	1205.1	12.0	1360.5	12.9
Imports	657.2	754.8	14.9	855.6	13.4	956.0	11.7	1080.1	13.0	1209.1	11.9	1350.9	11.7
Balance	−27.8	0.9		7.9		−0.5		−4.5		−4.0		9.6	
Developing countries													
Exports[c]	532.1	596.9	12.2	666.3	11.6	736.4	10.5	809.4	9.9	882.0	9.0	956.6	8.5
Imports	468.1	555.1	18.6	638.4	15.0	733.3	14.9	826.7	12.7	929.5	12.4	1037.5	11.6
Balance	64.0	41.8		28.0		3.0		−17.3		−47.5		−80.9	

Developing countries: non-oil													
Exports[c]	224.5	262.0	16.7	291.9	11.4	327.9	12.3	365.1	11.3	406.4	11.3	448.0	10.2
Imports	296.3	343.4	15.9	385.9	12.4	439.6	13.9	489.5	11.4	548.4	12.0	609.1	11.1
Balance	−71.3	−81.4		−94.0		−111.7		−124.4		−142.0		−161.2	
Developing countries: oil													
Exports[c]	307.6	334.9	8.9	374.4	11.8	408.4	9.1	444.2	8.8	475.6	7.1	508.6	7.0
Imports	171.8	211.7	23.2	252.5	19.3	293.7	16.3	337.2	14.8	381.1	13.0	428.4	12.4
Balance	135.8	123.2		122.0		114.7		107.1		94.5		80.2	
Centrally planned countries[d]													
Exports[c]	138.4	154.9	11.9	176.4	13.9	200.4	13.6	228.9	14.2	259.3	13.3	294.5	13.6
Imports	148.7	168.0	14.5	186.1	10.7	207.1	11.3	234.5	13.2	264.5	12.8	302.2	14.2
Balance	−8.3	−13.2		−9.7		−6.7		−5.7		−5.3		−7.7	
Rest of the world													
Exports[c]	163.4	198.3	21.3	188.3	−5.0	238.6	26.7	286.6	20.1	328.5	14.6	366.4	11.5
Imports	165.1	202.9	22.9	229.6	13.2	261.0	13.7	293.9	12.6	328.2	11.7	365.6	11.4
Balance	−1.7	−4.6		−41.3		−22.4		−7.3		0.3		0.8	
World exports	1869.9	2168.4	16.0	2468.3	13.8	2792.4	13.1	3146.6	12.7	3516.2	11.7	3915.8	11.4
World export price	3.3	3.7	13.0	4.0	8.0	4.3	7.6	4.6	6.8	4.9	6.5	5.1	5.5
World exports (real)[a]	578.2	588.4	2.6	620.1	5.4	652.1	5.2	688.2	5.5	722.4	5.0	762.6	5.6
World export price of fuel	10.9	12.1	11.0	13.3	9.9	14.5	8.5	15.6	7.7	16.7	6.9	17.7	6.1
World export of fuel (real)	40.9	39.3	−3.8	41.1	4.6	42.8	4.1	44.6	4.1	46.2	3.7	48.2	4.3

Table 10c – continued

	1986	1987	% Change	1988	% Change	1989	% Change	1990	% Change	1980–85e	1985–90e	1980–90e
13 LINK OECD countries[b]												
Exports[c]	2298.3	2559.6	11.4	2861.1	11.8	3188.3	11.4	3534.2	10.8	14.6%	11.5%	13.1%
Imports	2210.5	2435.1	10.2	2686.1	10.3	2956.7	10.1	3229.2	9.2	12.8%	10.1%	11.5%
Balance	87.9	124.4		174.9		231.6		304.9		21.6	184.8	103.2
US and Canada												
Exports[c]	588.9	656.2	11.4	734.9	12.0	823.3	12.0	909.6	10.5	14.4%	11.6%	13.0%
Imports	579.9	633.2	9.2	691.4	9.2	754.4	9.1	814.4	8.0	12.6%	9.0%	10.8%
Balance	9.0	23.0		43.5		68.9		95.2		-9.9	47.9	19.0
Japan and Australia												
Exports[c]	348.9	381.5	9.3	424.8	11.4	472.3	11.2	530.1	12.2	17.9%	11.0%	14.4%
Imports	279.6	304.1	8.8	330.2	8.6	358.9	8.7	386.7	7.7	12.8%	8.7%	10.7%
Balance	69.3	77.4		94.7		113.4		143.4		31.5	99.6	65.6
Rest of OECD												
Exports[c]	1360.5	1521.8	11.9	1701.4	11.8	1892.7	11.2	2094.5	10.7	13.9%	11.7%	12.8%
Imports	1350.9	1497.8	10.9	1664.6	11.1	1843.4	10.7	2028.2	10.0	13.0%	10.9%	11.9%
Balance	9.6	24.0		36.8		49.3		66.3		-0.0	37.2	18.6
Developing countries												
Exports[c]	956.6	1025.8	7.2	1094.3	6.7	1160.7	6.1	1216.7	4.8	10.6%	6.6%	8.6%
Imports	1037.5	1143.8	10.2	1261.6	10.3	1387.9	10.0	1524.8	9.9	14.7%	10.4%	12.5%
Balance	-80.9	-118.0		-167.3		-227.3		-308.1		1.6	-180.3	-89.4
Developing countries non-oil												
Exports[c]	448.0	490.2	9.4	539.4	10.0	594.2	10.2	649.6	9.3	12.6%	9.8%	11.2%
Imports	609.1	669.2	9.9	739.6	10.5	817.0	10.5	903.5	10.6	13.1%	10.5%	11.8%
Balance	-161.2	-179.0		-200.2		-222.8		-253.8		-110.7	-203.4	-157.0

Developing countries oil												
Exports[c]	508.6	535.6	5.3	554.9	3.6	566.5	2.1	567.1	0.1	9.1%	3.6%	6.3%
Imports	428.4	474.6	10.8	522.0	10.0	571.0	9.4	621.3	8.8	17.3%	10.3%	13.7%
Balance	80.2	60.9		32.9		−4.5		−54.2		112.3	23.1	67.7
Centrally planned countries[d]												
Exports[c]	294.5	326.8	11.0	365.3	11.8	406.6	11.3	448.9	10.4	13.4%	11.6%	12.5%
Imports	302.2	335.0	10.9	375.7	12.2	419.5	11.7	464.0	10.6	12.5%	11.9%	12.2%
Balance	−7.7	−8.1		−10.4		−12.9		−15.1		−8.1	−10.8	−9.5
Rest of the world												
Exports[c]	366.4	405.5	10.7	450.2	11.0	503.0	11.7	561.1	11.5	15.0%	11.3%	13.1%
Imports	365.6	403.7	10.4	447.4	10.8	494.5	10.5	542.9	9.8	14.7%	10.6%	12.6%
Balance	0.8	1.7		2.8		8.6		18.2		−15.1	6.4	−4.3
World exports	3915.8	4317.6	10.3	4770.8	10.5	5258.6	10.2	5760.9	9.6	13.5%	10.4%	11.9%
World export price	5.1	5.4	5.2	5.6	4.6	5.9	4.0	6.1	3.3	8.3%	4.5%	6.4%
World exports (real)[a]	762.6	799.4	4.8	844.4	5.6	894.9	6.0	948.8	6.0	4.7%	5.6%	5.2%
World export price of fuel	17.7	18.7	5.7	19.6	4.8	20.4	4.0	20.9	2.8	8.8%	4.7%	6.7%
World export of fuel (real)	48.2	49.7	3.1	51.5	3.6	53.4	3.8	55.6	4.0	2.5%	3.8%	3.1%

a Constant dollars measures have base 1970 = 1.0.
b Thirteen LINK OECD countries are: Australia, Austria, Belgium, Canada, Finland, France, Federal Republic of Germany, Italy, Japan, Netherlands, Sweden, United Kingdom and the United States of America.
c Measures are for merchandise trade, f.o.b.
d Includes only Eastern Europe CMEA and the USSR.
e Period averages are calculated as the compound annual growth rate of the last over first year projection.
Date of compilation: 18 June 1981.

Trade 10d Project LINK world trade summary: oil prices indexed to OECD export prices and OECD real output growth (US$billions)

	1980	1981	% Change	1982	% Change	1983	% Change	1984	% Change	1985	% Change	1986	% Change
13 LINK OECD countries[b]													
Exports[c]	1036.0	1219.0	17.7	1439.5	18.1	1622.7	12.7	1833.7	13.0	2070.3	12.9	2333.5	12.7
Imports	1090.0	1247.6	14.5	1431.1	14.7	1623.0	13.4	1845.0	13.7	2076.9	12.6	2327.2	12.1
Balance	-54.0	-28.6		8.5		-0.3		-11.3		-6.6		6.4	
US and Canada													
Exports[c]	268.5	305.9	13.9	374.6	22.5	429.0	14.5	479.3	11.7	534.0	11.4	600.4	12.4
Imports	293.2	334.3	14.0	387.0	15.8	443.6	14.6	503.7	13.5	563.7	11.9	627.9	11.4
Balance	-24.7	-28.4		-12.4		-14.6		-24.3		-29.6		-27.5	
Japan and Australia													
Exports[c]	138.1	157.1	13.8	200.1	27.4	235.1	17.5	272.9	16.1	320.0	17.3	356.3	11.4
Imports	139.6	156.8	12.3	182.9	16.6	213.1	16.5	244.8	14.9	279.6	14.2	314.3	12.4
Balance	-1.5	0.3		17.2		22.0		28.1		40.4		42.0	
Rest of OECD													
Exports[c]	629.4	756.0	20.1	864.8	14.4	958.6	10.9	1081.5	12.8	1216.3	12.5	1376.8	13.2
Imports	657.2	756.5	15.1	861.2	13.8	966.4	12.2	1096.5	13.5	1233.6	12.5	1385.0	12.3
Balance	-27.8	-0.5		3.6		-7.7		-15.1		-17.4		-8.2	
Developing countries													
Exports[c]	532.1	603.1	13.3	686.7	13.9	775.1	12.9	871.9	12.5	972.9	11.6	1081.6	11.2
Imports	468.1	557.0	19.0	645.0	15.8	747.2	15.9	850.0	13.8	964.7	13.5	1085.9	12.6
Balance	64.0	46.2		41.7		27.9		21.9		8.3		-4.3	

Developing countries: non-oil													
Exports[c]	224.5	261.4	16.4	289.9	10.9	324.5	11.9	360.3	11.1	401.2	11.3	441.6	10.1
Imports	296.3	342.5	15.6	383.3	11.9	435.1	13.5	483.4	11.1	542.0	12.1	601.5	11.0
Balance	−71.8	−81.1		−93.4		−110.7		−123.0		−140.8		−159.8	
Developing countries: oil													
Exports[c]	307.6	341.7	11.1	396.8	16.1	450.6	13.6	511.6	13.5	571.7	11.8	639.9	11.9
Imports	171.8	214.4	24.8	261.7	22.0	312.1	19.3	366.6	17.5	422.6	15.3	484.4	14.6
Balance	135.8	127.3		135.1		138.6		145.0		149.1		155.5	
Centrally planned countries[d]													
Exports[c]	138.4	155.2	12.1	177.6	14.4	203.1	14.3	233.4	14.9	266.5	14.2	304.7	14.3
Imports	146.7	168.1	14.6	186.5	10.9	208.1	11.6	236.4	13.6	267.8	13.3	306.5	14.5
Balance	−8.3	−12.9		−8.9		−5.1		−3.0		−1.3		−1.8	
Rest of the world													
Exports[c]	163.4	198.5	21.5	189.1	−4.7	240.3	27.1	289.6	20.5	333.5	15.2	373.6	12.0
Imports	165.1	203.1	23.0	230.4	13.5	262.8	14.0	297.2	13.1	333.9	12.4	373.8	11.9
Balance	−1.7	−4.6		−41.3		−22.5		−7.6		−0.4		−0.2	
World exports	1869.9	2175.5	16.4	2492.9	14.6	2841.1	14.0	3228.5	13.6	3643.2	12.8	4093.4	12.4
World export price	3.3	3.7	13.5	4.0	8.9	4.4	8.6	4.7	7.7	5.1	7.3	5.4	6.5
World exports (real)[a]	573.2	587.8	2.5	618.3	5.2	648.9	4.9	684.3	5.5	719.5	5.1	759.0	5.5
World export price of fuel	10.9	12.4	13.0	14.0	13.5	15.7	12.1	17.5	11.3	19.3	10.2	21.1	9.5
World export of fuel (real)	40.9	39.3	−3.9	41.0	4.4	42.6	3.9	44.2	3.9	45.9	3.6	47.7	4.1

Table 10d — continued

	1986	1987	% Change	1988	% Change	1989	% Change	1990	% Change	1980–85e	1985–90e	1980–90e
13 LINK OECD countries[b]												
Exports[c]	2333.5	2608.6	11.8	2930.5	12.3	3282.2	12.0	3669.8	11.8	14.9%	12.1%	13.5%
Imports	2327.2	2591.9	11.4	2896.3	11.7	3232.2	11.6	3593.5	11.2	13.8%	11.6%	12.7%
Balance	6.4	16.7		34.2		50.0		76.3		–7.7	36.7	14.5
US and Canada												
Exports[c]	600.4	672.0	11.9	755.8	12.5	850.1	12.5	947.1	11.4	14.7%	12.1%	13.4%
Imports	627.9	697.5	11.1	776.2	11.3	860.8	10.9	951.6	10.5	14.0%	11.0%	12.5%
Balance	–27.5	–25.4		–20.4		–10.7		–4.5		–21.9	–17.7	–19.8
Japan and Australia												
Exports[c]	356.3	392.1	10.0	439.8	12.2	491.7	11.8	557.8	13.4	18.3%	11.8%	15.0%
Imports	314.3	351.0	11.7	392.7	11.9	441.6	12.5	494.7	12.0	14.9%	12.1%	13.5%
Balance	42.0	41.0		47.1		50.1		63.1		21.6	48.7	35.1
Rest of OECD												
Exports	1376.8	1544.5	12.2	1735.0	12.3	1940.4	11.8	2164.9	11.6	14.1%	12.2%	13.1%
Imports	1385.0	1543.4	11.4	1727.5	11.9	1929.7	11.7	2147.2	11.3	13.4%	11.7%	12.6%
Balance	–8.2	1.1		7.5		10.6		17.8		–7.4	5.8	–0.8
Developing countries												
Exports[c]	1081.6	1191.1	10.1	1310.3	10.0	1440.0	9.9	1575.4	9.4	12.8%	10.1%	11.5%
Imports	1085.9	1207.9	11.2	1344.7	11.3	1494.9	11.2	1665.2	11.4	15.6%	11.5%	13.5%
Balance	–4.3	–16.7		–34.4		–54.9		–89.8		29.2	–40.0	–5.4
Developing countries non-oil												
Exports[c]	441.6	482.6	9.3	530.6	9.9	582.8	9.8	641.5	10.1	12.3%	9.8%	11.1%
Imports	601.5	660.8	9.9	730.1	10.5	805.1	10.3	895.4	11.2	12.8%	10.6%	11.7%
Balance	–159.8	–178.2		–199.6		–222.3		–254.0		–109.8	–202.8	–156.3

Developing countries oil												
Exports[c]	639.9	708.6	10.7	779.8	10.1	857.1	9.9	933.9	9.0	13.2%	10.3%	11.7%
Imports	484.4	547.1	12.9	614.6	12.3	689.8	12.2	769.8	11.6	19.7%	12.7%	16.2%
Balance	155.5	161.5		165.2		167.4		164.2		139.0	162.7	150.9
Centrally planned countries[d]												
Exports[c]	304.7	341.1	12.0	385.7	13.1	435.0	12.8	488.2	12.2	14.0%	12.9%	13.4%
Imports	306.5	341.5	11.4	386.5	13.2	436.1	12.8	488.6	12.1	12.8%	12.8%	12.8%
Balance	-1.8	-0.4		-0.8		-1.1		-0.4		-6.2	-0.9	-3.6
Rest of the world												
Exports[c]	373.6	415.4	11.2	464.0	11.7	521.7	12.4	586.9	12.5	15.3%	12.0%	13.6%
Imports	373.8	415.0	11.0	463.1	11.6	515.7	11.4	573.0	11.1	15.1%	11.4%	13.3%
Balance	-0.2	0.4		0.9		6.0		13.9		-15.3	4.2	-5.5
World exports	4093.4	4556.2	11.3	5090.6	11.7	5678.8	11.6	6320.3	11.3	14.3%	11.6%	13.0%
World export price	5.4	5.7	6.2	6.1	5.9	6.4	5.7	6.8	5.2	9.2%	5.9%	7.5%
World exports (real)[a]	759.0	795.2	4.8	838.7	5.5	885.3	5.6	936.1	5.7	4.6%	5.4%	5.0%
World export price of fuel	21.1	23.1	9.3	25.1	8.8	27.3	8.6	29.5	8.0	12.0%	8.9%	10.4%
World export of fuel (real)	47.7	49.2	3.0	50.9	3.5	52.7	3.6	54.6	3.7	2.3%	3.6%	2.9%

a Constant dollars measures have base 1970 = 1.0.
b Thirteen LINK OECD countries are: Australia, Austria, Belgium, Canada, Finland, France, Federal Republic of Germany, Italy, Japan, Netherlands, Sweden, United Kingdom and the United States of America.
c Measures are for merchandise trade, f.o.b.
d Include only Eastern Europe CMEA and the USSR.
e Period averages are calculated as the compound annual growth rate of the last over first year projection.
Date of compilation: 20 June 1981.

Table 11 Comparative simulations of global econometric systems under various oil price indexation scenarios (percentage deviations of real growth rates or levels of shock from baseline)

Economic grouping	FUGI GMEM[a]			LINK[b]		
	Scenario I[c]		Scenario II[d]	Scenario I[c]		Scenario II[d]
	1981	1982	1980-90	1981	1982	1980-90
Oil price (nominal)	12.2	0	3.6	12.5	0.9	4.0
Developed market economies (OECD)						
GDP	0.0	−0.2	−0.1	−0.4	−0.2	−0.2
PC	0.4	0.1	0.3	0.5	0.2	0.3
Exports	0.0	0.3	−0.1	−0.9	−0.3	−0.5
Imports	−0.1	−0.2	−0.2	−0.7	−0.4	−0.3
Trade balance[e] (f.o.b. US$billions)	−17.6	−6.4	−43.8 (1990)	−23.0	−25.0	−228.6 (1990)
Exchange rate (1975 = 100% US$)	0.0	0.0	0.0	—	—	—
Developing economies						
Non-oil exporters						
GDP	0.0	0.1	0.2	−0.6	−0.2	−0.4
PC	2.2	0.6	2.0	2.2	0.6	1.2
Exports	0.0	0.1	−0.1	−1.5	−0.4	−0.4
Imports	0.0	−1.0	−0.3	−5.1	−0.5	−2.0
Trade balance (f.o.b. US$billions)	−10.5	−8.9	−111.8 (1990)	0.0	0.0	−1.0 (1990)
Exchange rate (1975 = 100% US$)	0.0	−0.0	−1.8	—	—	—
Oil exporters						
GDP	0.0	−0.1	0.2	0.0	0.0	0.0
PC	−0.1	0.3	0.2	0.6	0.5	0.5
Exports	−1.1	−2.0	−0.5	0.7	0.2	1.4
Imports	0.0	2.8	0.6	5.6	0.2	1.5
Trade balance (f.o.b. (US$billions)	+28.6	+15.9	+163.8 (1990)	+20.6	+23.1	+218.4 (1990)
Exchange rate (1975 = 100% US$)	+ 0.0	−0.0	−1.9	—	—	—

For notes, see opposite.

The main results are shown in Table 13. It is estimated that a sharp decline in economic activity would occur in the industrial world in 1986, the year of the price increase, and that recovery would be fairly complete during the next few years, if the nominal oil prices were to be steady. The impacts on the oil-importing developing countries would, according to these calculations, be more severe and longer lasting; not only does growth slow down considerably, but also inflation would be much higher. Although trade balances for oil-importing developing countries worsen over the decade owing to terms of trade effects, according to LINK simulation for the baseline case, the oil shock does not enlarge it. At first this would seem to be counter-intuitive. However, in our simulations the volume of non-oil imports for these countries falls dramatically as the result of the oil shock, while the oil bill actually increases. In fact, this would have been the case for the oil shocks during the 1970s if there had not been a substantial increase in the inflow of capital (borrowing, aid from OPEC and OECD, IMF oil fund and so on) to these countries. In our simulations we have assumed that in the shock case the size of inflow of capital remains the same as in the baseline. This was done primarily to measure the full effect of the damage resulting from higher energy costs on these countries. We have not imposed exchange rate adjustments in this solution, for either the developed or developing countries. That adjustment could smooth the results in the

---

[a] FUGI Global Macro Economic Model, type IV 0 11-62 – June 1981 simulations (Prof. Akita Onishi, Soka University, Tokyo, Japan).

[b] LINK System – June 1981 simulations: LINK OECD Australia, Austria, Belgium, Canada, Finland, France, Germany, Italy, Japan, Netherlands, Sweden, United Kingdom and United States models.

[c] Scenario I: baseline for 1981 oil price set at \$32 per barrel and for 1982–90 = $\Delta \ln P_0$ (OPEC) = $\Delta \ln PX_{-1}$ (OECD); shock = for 1981 oil price set at \$40 per barrel and for 1982–90 $\Delta \ln P_0$(OPEC) = $\Delta \ln PX_{-1}$ (OECD), where P_0 = oil price and PX_{-1} = one period lagged export price.

[d] Scenario II: baseline = same as baseline in Scenario I; shock = $\Delta \ln P_0$ (OPEC) = $\Delta \ln PX_{-1}$(OECD) + $\Delta \ln GDP$(OECD), where GDP = gross domestic product in US dollars at 1970 prices. In the FUGI model, where exchange rates are allowed to change, oil prices also respond to changes in US\$ rate. PX in LINK refers to export price of manufactured goods (SITC 5–9); PX in FUGI refers to a weighted average of OECD export and consumer prices.

[e] Trade balances are deviation of shock from baseline in US\$billions, f.o.b.

Table 12 Oil price assumptions for mid-decade shock (percentage changes)

	Base case		Oil price shock	
	Nominal	Real	Nominal	Real
1981	25	8.8	25	8.8
1982	10	1.8	6.5	−0.5
1983	10	2.0	6.5	−0.5
1984	10	2.0	6.8	−0.5
1985	10	2.4	6.5	−0.3
1986	10	2.7	83.3	56.7
1987	10	2.8	0.0	−6.1
1988	10	3.0	0.0	−4.5
1989	10	3.1	0.0	−4.0
1990	10	3.0	0.0	−4.3
1981–90	11.4	3.14	11.4	3.27

medium term but not completely, since OPEC's currencies do not adjust, as discussed earlier.

For individual country estimates, the United Kingdom, United States, and Japan come close to zero growth in 1986, but pick up nicely, to trend values, soon afterward, assuming that it is only a one-year affair. Inflation responds significantly when the shock occurs in 1986, but subsides a great deal in most countries afterward, owing to the steadily declining *real* oil prices.

The oil price shock of 1974–75 in percentage terms was much larger but started from a lower price base. It caught nearly all industrial importing countries by surprise. This accounts, in some part, for the synchronized recession. By 1979, countries appear to have learned how to deal with expensive energy in short supply. Although the simulated shock of 1986 amounts to as much (or more) in dollar price increase, it has less impact on the world, and on most leading countries too, than in 1973–74, when everything was new, from the viewpoint of the policy problem. The new relative prices of energy have been accepted and economic activity has gone far in adapting to the situation. The industrial countries have managed their affairs so that they can start a long-term recovery at this time, but the oil-importing developing countries

Table 13 Effect of an oil price shock, 1986 (percentage changes)

	1980-85		1986/1985		1986-90	
	Base	Shock	Base	Shock	Base	Shock
LINK OECD						
Real exports	5.1	5.3	5.1	-0.5	5.0	5.2
Real imports	4.1	4.3	4.4	-0.4	4.5	4.6
Real GDP	3.5	3.6	3.1	1.2	3.0	2.9
Consumer price deflator	6.4	6.3	5.5	7.4	5.4	6.0
Trade balance[a]	-18.33	0.5	9.9	-151.5	51.8	-16.5
Oil-importing developing countries						
Real exports	2.7	3.2	4.9	-9.3	4.7	5.1
Real imports	2.4	3.4	2.6	-23.4	2.4	2.0
Real GDP	4.9	5.1	5.0	1.9	4.9	4.6
Consumer price deflator	20.5	19.9	11.5	25.0	10.9	11.5
Trade balance	-106.5	-107.4	-153.7	-139.3	-185.1	-180.8
Oil-exporting developing countries						
Real exports	0.2	-0.4	1.8	-9.7	1.1	0.0
Real imports	9.3	7.8	7.6	37.3	6.5	8.3
Real GDP	5.3	5.3	6.3	6.3	6.3	6.3
Consumer price deflator	10.0	9.7	6.9	7.5	6.7	6.8
Trade balance	142.4	125.6	144.4	284.8	141.0	197.9

[a] US$billions.

still face major problems in coping with their large balance of payments problems.

The results in this paper are worked out for the normal functioning of markets, even in the face of supply interruptions. We have not taken account of possible changes in the institutional structure of markets. There is presumably a sharing arrangement, developed by the International Energy Agency, that would come into force in the event of a major interruption in energy supplies. This sharing agreement may moderate the adjustment process of the developed countries beyond the results that we have estimated from market forces alone.

6 Recent Challenges to Keynesian Eonomics from the Supply Side, Rational Expectations, and Monetarism

Introduction

From the 1930s on, the Keynesian system became the mainstream model for theorizing about the macroeconomy and for implementing the policies to which this system of thought gave rise. Mainstream macroeconomics is now under attack by both theoreticians and policy-makers. I propose here to identify the sources of theoretical attack and to comment on the success, failure, or promise of alternative economic policies.

Naturally, my frame of reference will be the economy of the United States, but if this analysis is intended to be a contribution to the literature of macroeconomic theory, it should be formulated so as to refer to the whole world of industrial democracies. It is not going to be an exercise in applied econometrics, although such studies are wanted at this stage, but will attempt to be analytical, with some reference to quantitative measures.

When I was writing *The Keynesian Revolution*, almost forty years ago, I was an aspiring young economist taking issue with those of my elders who asserted that they could find nothing revolutionary in the Keynesian theory. They claimed either that all the relevant propositions for analyzing the macroeconomy were already contained in classical or neoclassical economics (Knight, Viner, Friedman, Simons, Hayek), or that they had already

Paper presented to the London School of Economics and Political Science as the Suntory-Toyota Lecture, January 1982.

created the same theoretical system, with appropriate policy recommendations (Frisch, Kalecki, Ohlin).

I now find myself taking issue with younger economists who claim that they have a new superior system of thought in various combinations of supply side economics (SSE), rational expectations (RE), and monetarism (M_i). These younger economists are flooding the scholarly journals and dominating the agendas of professional meetings with serious contributions to these three new branches of macroeconomics. The self-confidence of the advocates is exemplified in the following comment:

> Recently, however, most leading economic theorists have become persuaded that a different and superior procedure is provided by the hypothesis of rational expectations.

This remark comes from a response to a questionnaire circulated among selected American economists by the Joint Economic Committee of the US Congress seeking their opinions on the role of expectations in economics, and the quotation refers to the superiority of the rational expectations hypothesis over general lag distributions in own-values of expected magnitudes that are frequently used in mainstream econometric models, especially those with a Keynesian inspiration.[1]

In a similar vein, the exponents of SSE and M_i are challenging the Keynesian paradigm in macroeconometric model construction. The debate is shaping up as a contest in alternative econometric hypotheses, but the challenge is not narrowly a problem in econometric model specification and estimation; it is a challenge to the whole body of macroeconomic thought and it has cohesiveness because the challengers from the three sides have a convergent point of view: namely, that economic policy should be non-activist, non-interventionist. They all want very simple macro-rules, like an M_i rule, for example, and as much freedom as possible for the "magic of the market" to do its work, unimpeded by public authorities. At the present time, the three groups have some fundamental policy differences in the United States, but they

---

[1] Statement of Bennett T. McCallum in *Expectations and the Economy*, a volume of essays submitted to the Joint Economic Committee, Congress of the United States, December 11, 1981.

attempt to discount these differences because they are working toward a common goal of non-activist policy.

This characterization of the policy views refers mainly to the original proponents. Many young economists have taken up the theoretical lines of argument without having particular policy lines in view; this is the case, especially, with many of the younger generation who write serious papers on rational expectations.

Having made some brief introductory comments on the actors in the present doctrinal dispute, with some attempt to motivate their challenge, let me turn now to some factual background for the debate.

Some Casual Empiricism

A frequent point raised among the challengers is that Keynesian economic policy has failed. Keynesian policies are viewed as being inherently inflationary. After many years of implementation, they generated such inflationary conditions that slow growth and recession were the consequences, so that we have the unusual combination of rising prices and rising unemployment that is prevalent in a great part of the industrial world today. We call it "stagflation." The challengers claim, furthermore, that Keynesian-inspired econometric models were not able to foresee this development, and that the empirical manifestation of the theoretical system, as well as the policies, are therefore faulty.

A review of the quantitative record to examine this challenge and to provide a different interpretation of the facts is, accordingly, in order.

James Tobin has remarked to me that the very success of Keynesian economics has been a hindrance to its further development. Indeed, he felt that the original Keynesian thinkers were overwhelmed by success and were not challenged during the 1950s and 1960s to produce improvements that could have met some of the obstacles of the 1970s.

Before we concede shortcomings of the Keynesian system of thought about the macroeconomy, it will be useful to recall some of the accomplishments of the period since 1945. The numbers in Table 14 summarize some interesting developments. Viewed from

Table 14 World series (percentage changes)

	1950–60	1960–70	1970–80
World trade (1973 $US)	7.2	8.3	5.6
World GDP (1973 $US)	4.9	5.6	4.3
Inflation rate (market economies only, consumer prices)	2.9	4.6	11.0

today's perspective, the world economy went through an enormous development period from the end of World War II until the early 1970s. Keynesian economic policy, together with reconstruction and significant technical advances (jet aircraft, electronics, synthetic fibres, plastics, and others) propelled the economy in one of history's greatest advances in material living conditions, with very modest inflation. At the same time there was significant expansion of world trade. The Keynesian economic policy of demand management was very successful in contributing to excellent domestic economic performance in one country after another, and the Keynesian policies that culminated in the Bretton Woods system of fixed international parities helped bring about the strong expansion of trade, making the world economy much more interdependent in a liberal sense. This development was not uniform among major industrial countries or among economic groupings in the world, but in an overall sense it was a significant achievement.

Whenever there were disturbances, the mechanisms that were designed to supply the Keynesian medicine in a self-regulatory way went to work very effectively, although silently. Transfer payments, progressive tax systems, deposit insurance, agricultural price supports, and IMF advances all did their part. As long as the disturbances were confined to moderate ranges, these devices worked very well. On an international scale, cyclical movements were highly diversified, making for greater stability in the aggregate.

In the 1970s there was a breakdown of this smoothly working system. Why? The very success of Keynesian policies had kept the world economy from slipping back to the dismal situation of the interwar period and had introduced, by contrast, a period of sustained full employment that lasted more than two decades.

There were fluctuations; there were international differences in the attainment of full employment; but, by and large, it was a period of full employment. In Europe, North America, Japan, and Australia people could say that they had never "had it so good." Large parts of the developing world participated in the move toward economic betterment.

But prolonged periods of full employment, near the upper limit of capacity utilization, generated large inflationary pressures. In this respect, I believe that some recognition can go to a few anti-Keynesian economists who were able to foresee the inflationary prospects. After a Chicago seminar in the 1940s on postwar economic policies, Henry Simons remarked to me that Keynesian views would prevail but that we advocates would face significant inflation. In looking back on that discussion, it confirms to my mind that Keynesian economics was not enough, *not* that Keynesian economics was misleading or incorrect.

Just as some people forget that Keynes in part shaped the Bretton Woods system of fixed parities, and paid full attention to the problems of the open economy in an interdependent world, they also forget that he wrote a book entitled *How to Pay for the War*. The inflation problem is clearly one that can be perceived and tackled by Keynesian economics, although I believe that the analysis of inflationary war finance was not the appropriate theoretical scheme to apply fruitfully to the postwar expansionary boom.

I am still persuaded that the superposition of an extended Phillips curve (inverse relation between *wage change* and *unemployment*) on the conventional Keynesian system is the appropriate analytical tool. This extension must account appropriately for the time response mechanism in labor market adjustment, for changing socio-demographic composition of the work-force, and for changing institutional factors in the wage bargaining process in order to provide an adequate explanation of labor market pressures at full employment. But when Ronald Bodkin and I estimated in the early 1960s that it would require as many as 10 million unemployed in the United States to achieve wage and price level stability, labor market specialists thought that this figure was incredible. I regard it as realistic and indicative today of the lengths to which orthodox policy must set back the economy if it is to achieve its goal of low inflation through conventional measures of inducing recession and growth slowdown.

A second reason for the breakdown during the 1970s, apart from the sustained pressure on capacity operations, was the rapid sequential occurrence of large disturbances. Keynesian-type policies were adequate for the disturbances of the Korean War, the closing of Suez, and the Vietnam War, but those conflicts taxed the system to the limit. In fact, the beginning of the inflationary era in the United States is usually dated from the escalation of the Vietnam War in 1965. By 1971, the "dollar glut" had so displaced the "dollar shortage" that we in America had to close the gold window, devalue the dollar, and join in the replacement of fixed parities by the floating rate system. But the disturbances to follow were even more shocking – massive harvest failures, especially in the Soviet Union, the oil embargo, OPEC price hikes, the fall of the Shah of Iran, the Iran–Iraq War.

I do not agree that the Keynesian-type system is incapable of explaining the simultaneous occurrence of rising prices and rising unemployment in the 1970s. In simulations of the Wharton model, which is Keynesian-inspired if not simplistic textbook Keynesian, I have no trouble at all in generating responses to external shocks of high grain or fuel prices that show positive association between unemployment and inflation. It is an important analytical problem to determine how much of present stagflation is due to external disturbances, how much is due to years of Keynesian demand management, and how much is due to excessively lax monetary policies during the 1970s.

Every decade will have its disturbances, but those of the 1970s were unusually severe. I do not think, however, that they were severe enough to compromise the structure of the economy for modeling purposes. They did not invalidate the structures of the *mainstream* model, a term that I now prefer to *Keynesian* model. They can nevertheless be blamed for a good portion, probably the greater portion, of our present ills. Could orthodox policies have done better?

Consider Germany and Switzerland, often cited as paragons of wise finance and low inflation. They had important buffers in 1974–75 – namely, guest workers, who bore the brunt of unemployment. Germany did not successfully avoid high unemployment for long, and Switzerland has had to pay the price for low inflation in the form of slow growth. Both Germany and Switzerland have experienced significant increases in inflation during the past year or more.

Japan suffered high rates of inflation with recession after the first oil shock, but seems to have come out much better the second time round. But Japan's twin performances in achieving relatively low rates of inflation with moderately good rates of growth are due, in large measure, to aggressive export policy and highly restrictive wage policy, both fully consistent with the mainstream model.

Overly restrictive monetary policies during 1974–75 and 1980–81 in the United States and restrictive policies in the United Kingdom since 1979, inspired by other systems of thought, have not been validated. They have not indicated that a Keynesian way of thinking is wrong and that their type of domestic policy reactions to the disturbances of the 1970s could have produced better results. Both countries have suffered serious recessions with only moderate improvement in inflation. In both cases, wage restraint, as in Japan during the past two years, could have done a great deal to have improved the inflation record, without needlessly generating recessions, but policy-makers have chosen to challenge Keynesian-type thinking.

The lesson of the dismal record of the 1970s is not to replace our systems of thought or to renovate our inventory of policy instruments, but to build constructively on what we have in place. If the wage–unemployment relationship has become unfavorable to the implementation of stabilization policy, we should investigate the multi-dimensional extension to include labor force demographics, work aspirations of women, changing wage drift, and changing institutional features of the bargaining process. This is, in my opinion, far more fruitful than an immediate (knee-jerk) reaction to monetarism or some other simplistic explanation that necessarily requires a rethinking of macroeconomics. In the United States, the Wharton group of macroeconometric model-builders have fruitfully added energy and food detail to models in order to make better assessments of external shocks from these two sectors. To make better assessments from other sectors, too, where further shocks could occur, requires the elaboration of models to combine total input–output systems with macro-systems of final demand, income generation, and functioning of money markets.

In addition to external disturbances, problems arose during the 1970s in dealing with the physical environment, health, safety, and exhaustible resources (besides fuels). These I call structural problems, requiring structural policies. Macro-policies are surely inadequate to these challenges. No amount of degree of imposition of monetary rules, overall fiscal stringency, or general tax manipulation is going to address these structural issues. The addition of structural policies to deal with these specific sectoral issues requires the use of sectoral systems; that is why the Keynesian system is inadequate and needs extension. It is not because of the claims of the present array of challengers.

Theory

The Meaning of SSE

The students and readers of Marshall know better than anyone else that both blades of the scissors do the cutting. Keynes was a student of Marshall and does have an implicit supply side in his macro-system, even an explicit aggregate supply function. There is no doubt, however, that Keynesian economic policy has focused on aggregate demand management. The supply side of the Keynesian system needs to be brought more into the open and elaborated upon, but this is not the direction that SSE has taken in the United States today. There is overemphasis and concentration on large-scale, general tax cuts, as manifestations of supply side economics.

First, there is an intuitive impression that *marginal* tax rates have become oppressively high, to the point of obliterating incentives. The United States has gone less far in that direction than have other countries, such as the United Kingdom and Scandinavia. Large-scale tax reductions at the margin can undoubtedly improve incentives, but are they powerful; are they quick; do they have side effects? In principle, they are relatively easy to introduce into the Keynesian model. Labor supply should be made a function of real after-tax wage rates.[2] Similarly, interest rate effects on saving, investment, and liquidity preference should take account of marginal tax costs in accordance with the revenue statutes of the country being studied.[3]

Empirical studies in the United States indicate that there are some supply side effects, but that they are relatively small and stretched out over several years in achieving their full impact. Policy-makers in the Reagan administration have proceeded blindly, in the face of responsible professional warnings, to depend on this optmistic version of supply side economics by enacting large cuts in marginal tax rates spaced over three successive tax years. Adverse expectations were generated in the financial community about the size of public deficits, and interest rates rose astronomically because the Federal Reserve system, following monetarist operating rules, would not accommodate the financing of these deficits. There was no surge of labor productivity (from the labor supply effect), no sudden shift towards high savings, and no spurt in capital formation.

The result has, ironically, been that a serious unexpected recession has been generated by a combination of expectations, monetarism, and false reliance on supply side economics. The large deficits, the high interest rates, and the recession were predicted by the Keynesian-type models that were being criticized. Months before Wall Street recognized the problems of the deficit, operators of the three principal mainstream models testified before Congress that large deficits were being projected and that the administration's plan contained serious inconsistencies, but the government's preoccupation with challenging and dismissing the models led to the economic problems that we presently face.

To add to the irony, the administration now claims that it is extremely fortunate that statutory tax cuts are in place (July 1,

---

[2] This is a point of confusion in the early renditions of Keynesian economics. I do not think that there is any "money illusion" on the part of workers. Their penchant for indexing is strong proof to the contrary. My preferred versions of the Keynesian system keep the labor supply in real terms, but allow for mathematical inhomogeneity in carrying out the wage bargain in an extended Phillips curve process.

[3] This was done in the statistical estimation of Keynesian liquidity preference equations in the 1950s.

1982, and July 1, 1983) to fight the recession. This is purely a point of view of Keynesian economic policy and is being used by spokesmen who previously had said that the tax system should not properly be used to try to stabilize the macroeconomy; it should be used only to pay for the minimum necessary costs of government.

There is something to supply side economics, even to the populist version that rationalizes the present US government's policies, but there are no grounds for interpreting it as a challenge to Keynesian economics.

The Meaning of RE

The concept of expectations is old in economics, and it was hardly thought to be at variance with either the theory or practice of Keynesian economics. Macroeconometric models of Keynesian or other persuasion have long used expected values, certainly for more than thirty-five years. To a large extent, expected values have been indicated by lag distributions of own values, i.e.,

$$p_t^e = \sum_{i=0}^{n} \alpha_i p_{t-i} + u_t.$$

This is obviously just an approximation, but economic theory has had little to say about the specification of expected values and it seems plausible to argue that people looked at levels, changes, accelerations, and higher-order lags (histories) in order to fix the expected values of unknowns. Somewhat different lag distributions come about through assumptions of an adaptive adjustment mechanism to correct for recent disequilibrium.

A more advanced expression for expected values has been in the form of using quantified responses to questions in sample surveys. Wharton models, for example, have used investment expectations, consumer purchase expectations, more general consumer attitudes, and price expectations in model construction. They have not only used the response values for expected values, but have also tried to generate these magnitudes as endogenous variables in models. Many forward indicators of expectations, such as orders and housing starts, are also used as variables in mainstream macro-models.

Rational expectations are more stylized. In one interpretation, this theory assumes that economic decision-makers have at their disposal the same information as model-builders, policy-makers, and economic analysts and that they (economic subjects) use this information in the best possible way to form their expectations, just as model-builders, policy-makers, and economic analysts use it.

It makes sense to assume that people make use of many information sources, maybe even as many as are available, but to assume, whether implicitly or explicitly, that they use them in the same way as do professionals is wholly unwarranted or implausible. There is great variability in people's perceptions of the economic process, and to assume that they all typically go through the same techniques for information-processing is not justified. In some versions of the theory, it is assumed that economic subjects have the same model or come to the same conclusions as model operators in forming expectations as model projections, which seems ridiculous to me. I cannot imagine the ordinary citizen coming to my own conclusions, even indirectly, let alone following the same steps in reasoning that I follow. Also, I do believe that policy-makers and professional forecasters have some information sources that are wholly unknown to most people and certainly are much more quickly available to the professionals.

If economic subjects were generating expected values from the same model that we model operators are formally using, there would evidently be an identification problem in a linear world; so it is hard to see that there is much in the rational expectations model as far as structural estimation is concerned.

In yet another version of this theory, Robert Lucas has assumed that model parameters are functions of exogenous policy instruments. This is surely very special. It is a sensible generalization of the conventional macro-model to assume that parameters vary. That is one of the deep problems posing fruitful areas of future research, but there is no reason to believe that they are necessarily direct functions of the exogenous instruments. It is more reasonable to assume that they depend on cycle phase or follow some well-defined stochastic process, but I see no reason for saying that they depend on exogenous instruments, other than to make the contrived argument that people will always shift their behaviour so as to confound the authorities when new policies are implemented – to confound them in precisely such a way as to nullify the policy actions.

It is not too surprising that young economists have embraced the theory of rational expectations for much of their research in macro-dynamic economics. Economic theory has been relatively empty in the matter of specifying lag relationships or expectation relationships. Rational expectations, much like the engine of optimization, provide people with automatically generated processes. The main theorems of macroeconomics can now be reworked through the mechanism of rational expectations, and many research publications can be generated. Budding economists want a method for generating scholarly publications. Optimization methods provide specifications for the steady-state, or equilibrium, version of relationships, with dynamics left to the ingenuity of the investigator. Now that is changing.

The assumed lag distributions or parametric variations, either on the part of the conventional investigator or the rational expectations investigator, are based on hunches that cannot be directly verified. That is why I much prefer to go directly to the actors themselves and ask questions about expectations, both direct and indirect. It is not true that people distort their true findings or evade the issues; there have been great advances in survey methods over the years, and they have proved to be revealing in a variety of ways. Careful statistical study of sample survey responses have been beneficial in econometric model performance, especially for investment expectations, and they have not shown general support for the hypothesis of rationality, except in some restricted time periods. But it is not a matter of the accuracy of prediction of people's expressed expectations, it is a matter of being able to use them profitably in behavioral equations as indicators of decision variables upon which people act.

As far as macroeconometrics are concerned, the real test will be predictive ability, in a wide sense. In my professional lifetime, I have gone through one phase after another of potential break-throughs:

integrated accounts
quarterly data
monthly data

sophisticated methods of statistical inference
Bayesian statistical inference
cross-section data
control theory methods
high-speed computation.

They have contributed their bit, but none by itself has revolution-ized the subject or our ability to perform, except possibly the use of the computer and the provision of integrated accounts. There are gains to be made from this list and from a new list:

expectations
variable parameters
lag distributions.

But a breakthrough is hardly likely. While many of the avenues that seemed to be so promising in the past gave us more insight, they made, at best, only tiny contributions to better model performance. I confidently predict that the subject of rational expectations will simply be another element in this collection of things that did not provide a breakthrough.

Much of the scholarly debate has been about macroeconometric model performance and the new insight into model application brought about by the use of rational expectations, but this subject is not specifically econometric. It is an attack on the whole body of macroeconomic thought that forms the basis for activist policy. Some exponents of rational expectations simply argue that policy will not achieve its ends because people hold rational expectations. In the present policy debate about ways of halting inflation, proponents of RE have argued that if the government simply adopts a highly restrictive policy line, fiscal and monetary, and sticks to it with firm resolve, it will break the back of inflationary expectations. This would be strict orthodox policy. In the United State, it is interpreted as a policy to minimize the role of public action and public economic decision by cutting spending, cutting taxes, and adhering to a strict money supply rule.

This policy mix, together with increased military spending, generated expectations of budget deficits on Wall Street, and high interest rates. It was based on quite another scheme of reasoning by the administration, and the public hardly knew what to make of the whole situation. It appears to be a far cry from a situation in which many people are using the same body of information and generating the same expected values. It misfired to the extent of causing a recession that was wholly unexpected by public authorities. The President admitted this formally in a press conference.

The Meaning of M_i

Monetarism is both a theory for explaining the impact of money supply on economic activity and inflation, and a prescription for policy action by the monetary authorities. In its simplest form, the theory is based on a single relationship known as the quantity equation, which states that the stock of cash balances is proportional to the nominal value of transactions.

We shall confine our examination to the value added measure of transactions, say total GNP, that makes one side of the equation specific, although the doctrinal literature is not definitive on this point. The other side is optional, and this makes for great consternation on the part of all but monetarist enthusiasts. It could be, in succession

M_0, the monetary base
M_1, currency plus checkable deposits
M_2, M_1 plus some time deposits
$\vdots$
M_6, total financial credit

The quantity equation is

$$M_i v_i = pX$$

where v_i is the velocity (turnover rate) of M_i in purchasing the GNP (pX).

The quantity equation is not worth much as an analytical tool unless it contains some stable parameters. In its static form the only possible parameter is v_i, and the problem with uncertainty about the M subscript is that the stability of v_i is not independent of i. In a remarkable statistical study, Benjamin Friedman has found, from US data, that the time variability of v_i is a direct function of i. As he moves closer to a concept of total credit, he finds more stability in v_i. But for operating purposes, the monetary authority, in this case the Federal Reserve system, has more control over lower subscripted magnitudes than over higher subscripted magnitudes. Total credit is more meaningful in determining the level of nominal economic activity than is the monetary base, at the opposite end of the spectrum, yet the more meaningful magnitude is less controllable than M_0. In fact, the actual operations of the monetary authority affect the monetary base directly. They can control reserves and currency pretty well, but they have a difficult time controlling various types of deposits or credit instruments. When they feel that they have control over some particular M_i, the inventive financial system finds new instruments to befuddle the authorities. Financial practices are now undergoing an extraordinary process of technical change by opening new avenues for payments, holding monetary assets, or obtaining credit. The authorities have not done well in controlling the monetary aggregates in the face of introduction of

Eurocurrency balances
NOW accounts
money market funds
telephone transfer accounts
electronic funds transfers
credit cards
automatic tellers
saving certificates.

Recently, the Federal Reserve has been undershooting and overshooting its targets for M_{1B} and M_2.[4] It chooses to call this a stand-off. But if one looks at the history of operating policy, it is plain that, as soon as the authorities introduced monetarist rules of conduct (October 1979), they significantly destabilized the growth rate of M_{1B}. Their primary doctrine is that "some" monetary aggregate should be kept on a steady path, prudent for inflation control. This is definite policy, but it is, in a sense, no policy, because it is a fixed rule that is meant to be a substitute for all other policy. Decontrol of the economy to the fullest extent possible, and limitations of public spending and taxing are to accompany the monetary rule. That is the doctrinaire monetarist's

---

[4] The fact that M_i, in the United States, must carry a "B" subscript is indicative of the state of confusion in the definition of money supply. To add to the confusion, the "B" was dropped.

view of how the economy should be seen. It is, in fact, a policy of minimal discretionary action by public authorities.

The other side of the quantity equation needs some explanation. In its simple form, it appears that monetarist policy could, at best, determine the nominal value of GNP, the product of p and X. A monetarist view of the economy is that, if left alone, with a minimum of public interference, the economy would be quickly self-adjusting in such a way that fluctuations in X would be moderate in the neighborhood of full-capacity X. In this sense, X-fluctuations could be neglected and a direct proportional relation would exist between M_i and p if v_i were a stable parameter. From a policy point of view, it means that moderation in movement of M_i would lead to moderation of movement in p, or that inflation control policy should be M_i policy, regardless of the source of inflation. When the world was disturbed by the oil price shock in 1974–75, monetarists argued that the resulting inflation should be attacked through restrictive monetary policy.

Another view of monetarism is that it does not hold in the short-run; the economy is not necessarily quick in adaptation to a deviation from full capacity. Monetarist policy could, therefore, lead to depressed levels of X. By keeping the economy in prolonged recession or depression, there would eventually be a moderation in inflation. This is the view that the US administration has reluctantly come to accept, and it is apparently the view of the British government.

Several monetarists accepted this view that the simple form of the quantity equation would hold no better than the simple multiplier, or the simple acceleration principle. There are cyclical deviations about all these simple relationships, but do they hold in long-run or steady-state form?

Milton Friedman has investigated the generalized relationship

$$M_i v_i = \left(\sum_{i=0}^{s} w_i p_{-i} \right)^{\alpha} \left(\sum_{i=0}^{s} w_i X_{-i} \right)^{\beta}.$$

This attempts to establish a relationship with a time shape of response, with non-unitary parameter values (exponents). The right-hand side can now be interpreted as being composed of long-run price and long-run real output.

In this generalized form, the economists at the Federal Reserve Bank of St Louis in the United States estimated empirical relationships between nominal GNP on the one hand, and lag distributions of money supply and fiscal deficit on the other. They turned around the Friedman relationship and also included a fiscal measure, but with small perverse effect. As in the case of other high-correlation discoveries, the fundamental St Louis equation that symbolized a new surge in monetarism in the United States, and their entire model, met a just fate when faced with real-world phenomena. The Nixon administration's "New Economic Policy" of August 1971, the Soviet grain failure of 1972–73, and the oil embargo of 1973–74 were too much for the St Louis model. The operators fared badly in predictive testing and announced that their monetarist model was never intended for short-run analysis. It would hold only in the long run.

Many statistical series on M_i and GNP appear to move in accord with monetarist principles, in long-run averages with significant cyclical fluctuations. In simulating the Wharton econometric model over long stretches of time, the smooth, trend-like path of M_2 and GNP seem to move at a common rate of expansion. If we interpret these as two generated paths of endogenous variables, we note that they have a proportional association. This does not imply causation, much less policy instrumentation from one to the other, but it does seem to imply a monetarist expansionary association.

There is good reason for this long-run association, related to "third" factors − namely, the relation to the interest rate. A long-run simulation of the Wharton model has the property of putting the economy on a balanced growth path, along which the expansion rate settles down to a sustained long-term value of about 3 percent, with a nominal interest rate of about 8 percent and an inflation rate of about 5 percent. Velocity is not a constant parameter in this system, but is a function of the interest rate. When the rate settles down to a long-run value, velocity also settles down; so the proportionality relationship between M_2 and GNP is achieved.

The idea of making velocity a function of interest rate is decidedly non-monetarist; it is an empirical manifestation of Keynesian liquidity preference, but it is also inspired by Keynes's writings of the 1920s, where he notes that the Cambridge "k" (reciprocal of v) fluctuates in sympathy to changes in the interest rate. Also, the writings of Kalecki make velocity a positive function of the interest rate. The attempts of the US administration to generate a sustained growth of nominal GNP with a small growth in money supply brought about high values of v_{1B} (velocity), and the positive correlation between the interest rates and velocity prevailed. That is another way of looking at the reasons for recent high interest rates in the United states.

Truly, doctrinaire monetarism is single-minded. Some monetary aggregate is selected for the preparation of a growth target, and financial policy is geared to the attainment of that target. In the United States, the targets are stated jointly for M_1 or M_{1B} and M_2, but most attention, rightly or wrongly, is given the former. When one monetary aggregate growth rate has been below the accepted target range and another rate above the accepted target range, the Federal Reserve authorities act as though they successfully balance one error against another. Although they accept the principle of multiple targets as far as some components of M_i are concerned, they usually exclude interest rate or exchange rate targets. Monetarism, strictly interpreted, insists that there be adherence only to targets for money aggregates and that market rates be allowed to fluctuate where they will. This has brought extreme gyrations to interest rates and dollar rates, much to the consternation of many of our trading partners.

There is no good reason why a more general approach should not be taken, based on a loss function that gives appropriate weights to target deviations for market rates as well as for expansion paths of M_i. This would be in the spirit of the approach of control theory, which seeks to minimize a general loss function, subject to the system constraints. This would be an ideal field to experiment with the relaxation of monetarist dogma and extend the target space to some new dimensions.

While I side with those econometricians who would stop short of direct use of control theory results, at the present state of knowledge, in the policy formation process, I do recognize that there are some highly suggestive and useful results from control theory analysis that can be put to work in today's economic environment. One result that has been established by William Brainard and Leif Johansen is that control theory optimization programs for the economy in many cases call for less active use of instruments the greater is the degree of uncertainty about the validity of the constraint system. That is to say, the less sure we are about the precise functioning of the macroeconomy, the more cautious we should be in moving about economic policy instruments.[5] This is far different from saying that we should simply rely on the "magic of the market" and try to keep M_i under control, but it does show that, from quite another approach and philosophy of the functioning of the economic mechanism, we were independently coming to the viewpoint of seeking steadiness and moderation in the application of economic policy.

Before reaching the state at which "magic of the market" is applicable, very large changes in fiscal instruments are being proposed. Budget slashing on both the expenditures and revenue sides is unusually large. In the short run, this would seem to run counter to the Brainard–Johansen implications from control theory analysis.

Although the Reagan administration in the United States and the semi-independent Federal Reserve system praise the virtues of steadiness in economic policy, they actually are being forced by circumstances to reappraise their policies and instrumentation radically, on very short notice. Within less than one year, the administration has had to shift from contemplation of zero budget deficits to deficits approaching $200 billion and, correspondingly, to seek drastic changes in its fiscal policies. Similarly, the Federal Reserve has had to shift from policies that kept M_{1B} below target to more expansionary policies that occasionally appear to be on a runaway course. This is because SSE, RE, and M_i analyses were unusually misleading in 1981. It indicates to me that they are working with the wrong models, for all the reasons outlined above, and especially because their errors led to projections that are strongly inconsistent. Earlier in 1981, we often heard the remark that forecasts were relatively unimportant, that the important thing was to get on with the fiscal and monetary reforms. But flawed forecasts have upset the whole program and generated an unexpected and unwelcome recession.

---

[5] This interpretation is for the normal case, but loss functions and models can be constructed so that optimal policy calls for greater rather than less use of policy instruments in the face of uncertainty.

Extensions of the Keynesian System

Supply side economics, rational expectations, and monetarism are not empty concepts; it is simply a case of their being misapplied or seriously overstated. They do not, in my opinion, invalidate Keynesian economics, but they can be used in order to extend the Keynesian system to a point at which it will become more useful for the final quarter of the twentieth century. Professor Hicks has asserted that the third quarter of this century has been the age of Keynes; the problems have now changed, but I believe that the system needs to be adapted, not scrapped, during these closing decades. These remarks apply to both theory and policy.

In Chapter 3, I have argued for the forging and implementation of the Keynes–Leontief system. This is the contribution of SSE, properly interpreted. It has been under way for some time, long before the convergence of the populist SSE proponents of the Reagan administration in the United States and the implementation of their reckless spree of tax-cutting. The econometric model-building inspired by Ragnar Frisch in Norway and maintained by his successors, particularly Lief Johansen, already went in the direction of putting together the Keynes–Leontief system. Similar exercises have been undertaken by the Wharton group in the United States and by Richard Stone's Cambridge group in the United Kingdom. Other systems of this type are available elsewhere in the world. This is the *true* contribution of SSE, but it is complementary and not contradictory.

From the standpoint of econometric methodology, one of the most important lines of development is to improve our knowledge of the time shape of economic reactions, that is, the estimation of dynamics in the macroeconomy. This is where rational expectations may be called upon to help in the specification of economic relationships. Rational expectations are very special, and it is doubtful that macroeconomic analysis should tie itself to that restrictive view to any significant extent. The entire discussion has, however, highlighted the issue of the formation of expectations, and their importance in economic theory or policy. In many respects this is nothing new, but it is useful to have the points emphasized again. The end result is likely to be that much more attention will be paid to the dynamics of expectation formation and the role of lag distributions in economic models.

As for monetarism, discussions of this subject have brought home the point that money matters, if not the point that *only* money matters. It is fair to say that most macroeconomic analysis and most econometric models pay a great deal more attention to the monetary sector than ever before. This has been a healthy development and was under way before the present ascendancy of monetarism. If we assume that the linking of the input–output accounts with the national income and product accounts has been successfully completed, with the Keynes–Leontief model as one of the outcomes, I would say that the next step forward will come when the flow-of-funds accounts have been equally well linked with the other two accounting systems, with the emergence of an expanded money and credit system of macroeconometric models that explains the supply–demand balances between the main credit instruments. This phase of the analysis has already been implemented in the Wharton model, but the final step to incorporate the simultaneous determination of the whole spectrum of interest rates still needs to be completed.

On the theoretical side, therefore, we can accommodate SSE, RE, and M_i in the extended Keynesian system. What does this mean for economic policy? Is there an alternative to Keynesian macro-demand management, on the one hand, and neo-conservative policy of orthodox monetary and fiscal restraint, relying eventually on the "magic of the market," on the other hand? I think that an alternative exists, and I would call it implementation of structural policy, superimposed on well organized macro-demand management. A major ingredient of this type of policy is known as *industrial policy.*

The objectives of industrial policy are to raise productivity growth and to move the competitive position of each country toward greater efficiency. In looking at past performance, I would say that Japanese industrial policy of the 1960s was eminently successful, and it appears that the disruptive effects of the 1970s have been absorbed, preparing the economy for a new round of industrial policy in the 1980s. Similarly, I believe the French indicative planning was also successful as an industrial policy in the 1960s. It remains to be seen whether the new directions for French industrial policy are going to be as successful as previous schemes, but while we cite in the French and the Japanese cases successful examples of industrial policy. There are failures, and this course is chancy. I believe that the United States is very well situated for implementing a successful industrial policy.

The Reagan administration in the United States came to power on the basis of promises that we would not have to go through painful recessionary adjustments, with rising unemployment, in order to bring down the rate of inflation. That is plainly false, as we have the recession unfolding before our very eyes, and unemployment rose. A careful and well considered industrial policy, together with other structural policies dealing with environmental issues, demographic issues, and similar sectoral or micro-problems, offers an alternative. These fundamental policy changes are medium-term and require two or three years before their beneficial effects should begin to show through, but the short-run transitional problems for dealing with the immediate recession can be addressed through complementary demand management policies. Thus, this analysis is not empty. As well as criticizing present tendencies in macroeconomic thought, I believe that there are viable alternatives. Economic policy should not stop at national borders. I would strongly support steps toward the international coordination of policies. At summit meetings, the heads of state proclaim nice principles for economic cooperation of a coordinating sort, but they seldom follow through with effective coordinated action.

Keynes proposed an international economic system that would permit individual countries to adopt autonomous domestic policies that were kept in line with international objectives. The challengers to Keynesian thinking in the United States have effectively prevented summit partners from pursuing autonomous domestic policies to alleviate recession. A combination of monetarist operating procedures by the Federal Reserve and miscalculations of supply side effects, with expectations, on the real economy generated unexpected fears of large deficits, together with extraordinarily high interest rates. These appeared in the world economy at a time when the appropriate policy for many European countries, the United Kingdom, Canada, and Japan would have been to bring down interest rates; but to have done so in the face of high rates in the United States would have generated financial capital flight and exchange depreciation of other currencies against the dollar. The movements in exchange rates would have exacerbated inflationary problems; therefore this lack of coordination of monetary policies has been perverse for the world economy and occurred in an anti-Keynesian international environment — anti-Keynesian from the viewpoint of domestic policy, and anti-Keynesian from the viewpoint of international institutions. The attempt to dismantle Keynes's last contribution to economics, the design of the Bretton Woods system, has thus led nations into a trap that the system was designed to prevent, and the policies that led to this interest rate confrontation were the anti-Keynesian policies of SSE, RE, and M_i.

7 Economic Laws

It is very difficult, and may well not be possible, to find better available statements about the concept of economic laws than those in Marshall's *Principles*, Chapter III, entitled "Economic Generalizations or Laws."[1] Marshall observed that economic science is based on the same considerations and procedures that are used in other sciences, but he contrasted economics with "exact sciences." He also remarked:

> A science progresses by increasing the number and exactness of its laws; by submitting them to tests of ever increasing severity, and by enlarging their scope till a single broad law contains and supersedes a number of narrower laws, which have been shown to be special instances of it.

In many respects economic research proceeds in this way, but we economists find it very difficult to come to definitive decisions along the way about which laws to reject or accept, and we have a hard time establishing a single broad law. It is my opinion that the most important feature giving rise to economic science's lack of decisiveness is our inability to perform controlled experiments on a comprehensive replicated level. In this respect, we acknowledge unfavorable comparisons between the inexactness of economics and other social sciences, on the one hand, and natural sciences, on the other.

---

[1] A. Marshall, *Principles of Economics* (London: Macmillan, 1936), 8th ed., 29–37.

Experimentation is very important, but it is not the whole of the comparison. Marshall makes a comparison between the sciences of the tides (inexact) and the laws of gravitation (exact), and indicates that economics is akin to the former. But a more frequent modern comparison that is relevant for economics is between meteorology or seismology, on the one hand, and astronomy on the other. Inaccurate predictions are made about weather and earthquakes, while accurate predictions are made about the movements of the heavenly bodies. In all three cases there is no opportunity for controlled experimentation, yet the differences in precision are great.

Economic prediction is, in many respects, similar to weather prediction. The comparisons with seismology are more recent, but I have an intuitive feeling that we make better predictions of economic phenomena than seismologists do of earthquakes. The problem with weather prediction is that a large component in the end result comes from atmospheric turbulence. In the same sense, the residual random disturbance in economic relations accounts for a large part of our inaccuracy of prediction. In economics, as in meteorology, the noise-to-signal ratio is inherently large, while in astronomy it is small; therein lies the reason for the discrepancy in predictive performance.

Marshall spoke of economic laws as *tendencies* rather than as precise causal statements. His frame of reference was insightful, but general and logical. I hope to be more specific and empirical in trying to indicate just what it is that economists can assert with the authority of laws. I shall try to cover a variety of cases, but there is no thought of being comprehensive.

Some Great Ratios

A number of years ago, I tried to put together a self-contained macro-model (simultaneous equation system) of the economy as a whole by considering only a few ratios that economists use:

the savings ratio (rate)
the capital–output ratio
the wage share
the velocity ratio (quantity equation of money)
the labor participation ratio.

Economists often analyze the economic situation as though some, or all, of these ratios are stable parameters (constants).

The US savings ratio hovered around 10 percent for a long time, but has more recently been lower, fluctuating near 5 percent. This low value is frequently cited as being responsible in part for the present high interest rates and poor rate of growth in the United States. A high savings rate has been a factor in Japan's amazing success in economic growth. There is wide variation in the size of the rate across countries, however, and it is hardly a stable ratio in the short run. If the tendency toward constancy of the savings rate is to have any standing as a law of economics, it would have to be as a long-run proposition — say, the savings rate averaged over a decade or more. Some economists make this a central point of their analysis, but it is not widely enough accepted or established to be classified as a basic law of economics.

The same may be said of the capital–output ratio (or the crude acceleration principle of investment when it is put in change form). It is not sufficiently stable. But the share of wages in total production does seem to exhibit more empirical regularity. Paul Douglas implied this in his lifetime investigations summed up under the heading, "Are There Laws of Production?"[2] Wage–price guideline programs, which may yet see their day in more comprehensive implementations of incomes policies, are, in a sense, derived from inversions of the constancy of labor's share.

Personally, I have more faith, as an empirical economist, in the constancy of labor's share for the interpretation of inflation than in the quantity theory of money, which relies on the constancy of the velocity of circulation of money. The foundations of monetarism, now popular in the formation of economic policy in many parts of the world, rely on the stability of some form of velocity, and I would side with President Frank Morris of the Federal Reserve Bank of Boston, who argues that the concept of money is undergoing such great change that the monetarist rules do not apply, especially in day-to-day monetary management.[3] His argu-

---

[2] Douglas' presidential address to the American Economic Association was more positive than that of others, for he genuinely believed that economists could say something about the laws of production: *American Economic Review* 38 (1948): 1–41.

[3] Related findings of Benjamin Friedman of Harvard and policy arguments of Anthony Solomon of the Federal Reserve Bank of New York add much weight to the inference of instability of the monetarist laws.

ments are quite contemporary, but I believe that velocity has not been stable in the past.

Principles of demography and economics together are needed to explain movements of the labor force and participation rate. So many surprises in both the short and long run have occurred in economists' expectations about unemployment as a result of changes in labor force growth that we can have little confidence in the stability of the participation rate. First it was the baby boom; now it is the aspirations of working women that are cited as reasons for unusually high rates of unemployment.

Generally speaking, the Great Ratios are not stable enough to qualify as economic laws, except possibly the wage share of production, although they are interesting for use in crude speculative analysis with small models of scholarly or pedagogical nature. By averaging or smoothing the ratios, they may show more stability, but generalizations into dynamic relations with steady-state properties or as multivariate relations within the context of larger complete systems may lead to greater stability. For example, the present controversy about the validity of monetarism rests not entirely on the stability of velocity ratios, but also on the stability of generalized equations for the demand for money. It is my assessment, though, that even with these generalizations, the main principle of monetarism does not qualify as an economic law. I would not say either that the large-scale econometric models that my associates and I put together as systems for prediction qualify. Our models contain many components that may qualify as economic laws, and I believe that they provide the best means available at this time for charting our economic future, but I would not elevate the status of the Wharton model to that of a collective economic law: it is too uncertain and tentative, even though it has the best forecasting record of any system or approach that has been documented for systematic testing.

Some Economic Laws

What *are* some economic laws that can be accepted as having stood the test of time? Let us take Pareto's Law of Income Distribution as an example. Pareto observed that there is a tendency for individual incomes to be distributed so that the logarithm of the number of persons with income in excess of a given level is a negative linear function of the logarithm of that income level. This is an elegant and simple law of income distribution and can be used to good advantage in many analytical studies, but it does not hold on a universal scale – across countries and time periods. It has not been found to hold for the entire range of the income distribution, but it does hold on a broad scale for upper-income groups. In a restricted sense, it could qualify as a law of economics. Interesting interpretations have been put forward to show how people's movements among income classes tend to generate the Pareto law, but these analytical arguments are usually based on controversial assumptions. Taking Marshall's views of economic laws as general tendencies, we can say that Pareto's Law of Income Distribution or various complementary laws (for example, for the lower tail) can be considered as economic laws.

Another old law has more substantiation, namely Engel's Law of Food Expenditure – the fraction of incomes spent on food decreases as the level of income rises. This law is not very specific. It does not say how fast this ratio falls. But the general statement of the law, with varying numerical parameters for different countries, was found to hold uniformly by Hendrick Houthakker on the occasion of the centenary of the formulation of the law. To this very day, the family expenditure–income data for the United States, United Kingdom, and other major countries clearly show a falling tendency for the fraction of income spent on food as we move up the income scale.

Many decades after Engel formulated his law of food expenditure, J. M. Keynes stated a fundamental psychological law about total consumer expenditure. He said that consumers, in the aggregate, would spend on consumption only a fraction of an increase in income. In more technical terms, he asserted that the marginal propensity to consume is positive but less than unity. The *magnitude* of the marginal propensity to consume varies from situation to situation, but as far as I know, it is always less than unity. The general statement holds. A stronger law – that aggregate consumption depends only on aggregate income, either contemporaneously or with a distributed time lag – is not always invalidated, but the strict Keynesian proposition, like Engel's proposition, can stand as a law.

A stable savings ratio is a more specific law than Keynes'. The early researches of Simon Kuznets suggested, from an empirical point of view, that US consumers saved about 10 percent of their income, particularly when smoothed into decade numbers.[4] This empirical regularity prompted Milton Friedman to formulate his highly structured Permanent Income Hypothesis that long-run consumer expenditures or savings are proportional to long-run income. The Permanent Income Hypothesis has been provocative and has stimulated much research activity, but cannot be said to have withstood the test of time to qualify as an economic law. Data of the last two or three decades cast doubt on the stability of the savings–income ratio. In a similar way, Milton Friedman's restatement of stability of the velocity ratio into long-run money demand functions has not been established as an economic law. In fact, the instability of money demand relationships, as indicated above, brings into question the entire monetarist theory of the macroeconomy.

The laws of economics that have been discussed so far involve some behavioral principles, and if human beings decide to vary their behavior from average observed practice, the laws may be upset. But other laws hold in economics, by definition. Some are implied accounting balances and, in that sense, nothing but truisms. They may not, however, be evident, especially to the non-professional; therefore, it is meaningful to give them the elevated status of law. Walras' Law, called by that name, is essentially an accounting identity. Put one way, it states that the incomes paid to factors for producing all the goods and services marketed should equal the value of the goods sold, both consumer goods and producer goods (investment). In contemporary social accounting systems, this relationship routinely appears in the tables of correspondence between the national income and the gross national product (or expenditure). After some institutional items of reconciliation, we find that the GNP should equal the national income (paid to the factors of production), but there is a *statistical discrepancy* that arises because all the items of Walras'

---

[4] A stable national savings ratio, encompassing personal, business, government, and net foreign savings, has been called Denison's Law, but it is no more solidly established than is Kuznets' earlier observation on personal incomes.

Law are measured independently and imperfectly. In a logical sense, the law should hold exactly, but in an empirical accounting sense it holds inexactly. At the present time, the United States has a GNP value of about $3,000 billion, and the associated statistical discrepancy is estimated within a range of no more than plus or minus $10 billion.

Similarly, on a world scale, total imports should equal total exports, when measured in common (*numeraire*) units of valuation. In analogy with scientific laws, this accounting identity may be called a *law of conservation*, in the sense that no goods get lost in accounting for the trade that moves from one country to another. Again, measurement is imperfect, and separate accounting for imports and for exports leaves us with a world discrepancy of some $20 billion or more, associated with a world trade total of about $2,000 billion.

A law of roughly the same vintage as Walras' Law is Say's Law of Markets. It says, optimistically, that everything that gets produced will get sold, or that "supply creates its own demand." Philosophically, it could be interpreted as asserting that supply motivates economic activity. During the Great Depression, this point of view was strongly challenged by Keynes and his followers, who claimed that demand was the driving force. In the depressed conditions of the interwar period, the Keynesian point of view was undoubtedly more correct, but this position is being challenged today by supply side economics. The adherents of the latter school have not openly advocated the acceptance of Say's Law, but occasionally their arguments suggest that they believe in it. It would be stretching the imagination, however, to say that Say's Law has been verified or validated. While we can accept Walras' Law as an accounting identity that holds in practice, to the extent of our powers of observation, we cannot cite empirical support that is widely accepted as validating Say's Law. Nor can we, in any sense, claim that "demand creates its own supply."

It is not a case of one view or the other; both supply and demand aspects are simultaneously relevant. Marshall wisely noted that both blades of a scissors do the cutting, and we should not look to the supply side of economic life exclusively for insight into the workings of the system, any more than we should look solely to the demand side. But the *law of supply and demand* does have wide acceptance. It is based on the assumption and observation of a tendency of markets to get cleared, by finding a price that brings supply and demand into balance. In a more realistic and dynamic statement of this law, we can say that when supply exceeds demand in a given market, price in that market tends to fall in an attempt to bring about a balance between supply and demand. Conversely, when demand exceeds supply, price tends to rise. The law is not quantitative in the sense of saying how much, or how fast, price will change in the face of an imbalance between supply and demand; that will depend on the economic motivations of the particular consumers and producers in the market being examined.

Every day there are literally millions of transactions going on everywhere illustrating this dynamic law. But it can be obstructed. Price controls, freezes, and guidelines halt its working or modify it. To give a contemporary example that all can appreciate, in the present situation in the world oil market, a global oil glut is often referred to. Supply exceeds demand in this market at the present time, and there is correspondingly a tendency of prices to fall. In the past several years, the OPEC nations have largely fixed the price of oil, particularly in the period after the embargo of 1973. But sideline observers kept saying that the laws of economics would work, and gradually they have assumed more importance in the world oil market. By now, we are seeing the law of supply and demand at work, with prices falling in order to wipe out a condition of excess supply. However, if the OPEC nations are successful in restricting output significantly, for a protracted period of time, they will be able to eradicate the present situation of excess supply, and the price of oil could resume its upward path again, but this would be a path determined by the laws of economics and not governed by religious fervor or political opportunism.

Walras' Law and the law of supply and demand (leading to market clearing) are both components of larger systems — mathematical systems of simultaneous equations — which show that in equilibrium a freely competitive economy produces an optimal solution. This solution is optimal in the sense that it produces a state of affairs in which no economic agent can be made better off without simultaneously causing another agent to be worse off.

We call this situation one of *Pareto optimality*. This, of course, is not to be confused in any sense with Pareto's Law of Distribution, but is an analytical and logical proposition about economic behavior. We cannot easily, perhaps never will, observe an economy in a state of competitive equilibrium, and cannot test the existence of a condition of Pareto optimality. The principles of a competitive economy are useful in guiding our thinking and understanding of the system; they form the intellectual base of "trust busting," but they are not one of the economic laws that I am talking about. The laws of supply and demand can be estimated statistically, and Walras' Law is measured rather closely in our social accounting tabulations, but the principles of optimality are not observable or testable in the same sense.

In the field of international economics, a rich assortment of economic propositions has developed, and I shall draw on three of them for some comment. The first to be considered is the doctrine of comparative costs. It is stated not as a law, but as a doctrine that shows the gains from free trade, much as the doctrine of optimality derives the analysis of the working of a competitive domestic economy. Free competition and free trade are both conditions for the existence of optimality.

> The doctrine of comparative costs maintains that if trade is left free each country *in the long run* tends to specialize in the production of and to export those commodities in whose production it enjoys a comparative advantage in terms of real costs, and to obtain by importation those commodities which could be produced at home only at a comparative disadvantage in terms of real costs, and that such specialization is to the mutual advantage of the countries participating in it.[5]

The statement of the doctrine by J. Viner is clearly in the spirit of Marshall's concept of law of economics.[5] He speaks of *tendencies* that prevail in the *long run*.

In principle, costs could be measured, together with imports and exports, for a number of countries. Statistical measures of their mutual bilateral trade in association with their comparative

---

[5] Jacob Viner, *Studies in the Theory of International Trade* (New York: Harper, 1937), 438 (italic in original).

costs could validate or refute this proportion. In treating this doctrine as an economic law, it would have to be tested on a broad scale. Cost estimation is difficult, and many bilateral flows are to be considered simultaneously in order to come to a comprehensive conclusion.

A number of country pairs have been investigated for various industry groupings. In a recent dissertation, completed at the University of Pennsylvania, Toshiko Tange estimated production relations and costs in a number of manufacturing industries (2-digit groupings) for the United States and Japan respectively. She found a high correlation between export activity and cost efficiency, thus lending support to the doctrine. In looking casually at trading activity around the world, I would say that the long-run tendency predicted by the doctrine does exist.

A related proposition, or theorem, of international economics concerns relative availability and use of factors of production in relation to trade flows and specialization. It is known as the Hecksher–Ohlin theorem. In general terms, it states that a country tends to export the goods that intensively use the factors of production with which it is abundantly endowed and import those goods that use the factors with which it is poorly endowed. Paul Samuelson extended these propositions with a factor price equalization theory: that goods move, if markets are freely competitive, between countries, tending to bring factor prices into mutual equality.[6]

Like the laws of comparative advantage, the theorems about international specialization and price equalization are logical propositions that are hard to describe or verify empirically. They depend on very strict assumptions about competition, free mobility, availability of information, and similarity of tastes and preferences among countries. Also, they are carefully proved for the two-good, two-country case, which is only indicative of the workings of a multilateral system of general equilibrium. The strict assumptions are not met in practice, yet there is a feeling among many, if not most, economists that actual conditions are close enough to those assumed that an underlying tendency exists to satisfy the conclusions.

---

[6] P. A. Samuelson, "International Trade and the Equalization of Factor Prices," *Economic Journal* (June 1948).

In a highly provocative and stimulating statistical study, Wassily Leontief showed that the United States' trade patterns did not satisfy intuitive feelings about the workings of the Hecksher–Ohlin theorem.[7] He found that the United States exported products with relatively high labor content and imported those with relatively high capital content. Intuition would have expected the opposite.

From the point of view of documentation from widely accepted empirical studies, we cannot put the logical propositions about trade in the form of economic laws, but there is an analogous kind of proposition, known as the doctrine of purchasing power parity, that does come closer to being accepted as a fundamental law of economics in my sense. Purchasing power parity (PPP) claims that exchange rates between currency pairs move in the same proportion as relative rates of inflation in the two countries (or in one country against a weighted combination of countries in figuring both exchange valuations and relative inflation rates). This doctrine can be stated in terms of comparative cost changes. When stated in terms of export price changes, it can be interpreted as the law of one price – namely, that the price of an internationally traded good should be the same anywhere in the world, when price is compared in a common currency unit of account. Of course, transport and other institutional differences can exist.

Many careful students of international economics have studied the statistics of exchange rates and price movements between countries, only to conclude that PPP does not hold. In my opinion, these studies are too specialized, looking only at a pair of countries, at one time, and at some particular commodities. A few of these studies have covered long historical episodes, but recently most have concentrated on the period since 1973, when the present floating system of exchange rates came into being.

Short-run variations in exchange rates are related to many things, such as interest rate differentials, reserve positions, payments balances, capital flows, and international psychological tensions. But inflation differentials are also important, and in the long run are the dominant factors that PPP says that they ought

---

[7] Wassily Leontief, "Domestic Production and Foreign Trade: The American Position Re-examined," *Proceedings of the American Philosophical Society* (September 1953).

to be. In a fresh approach to this issue, some of my colleagues on Project LINK and I have found that PPP does hold – with annual statistics, over long stretches of time (about a decade or more), and across countries. Our investigations are for price indexes averaged over many commodities, and recognize that some countries may show greater sensitivity of exchange rate changes to inflation differentials than PPP indicates, while others may show less sensitivity. Our findings are truly those of a tendency, in the Marshallian sense. Figure 4, consisting of a scatter plot of percentage changes in dollar exchange rates against percentage changes in export prices relative to US export prices, shows that there is definitely a relationship. On average, it is close to the strict PPP relationship, which is the negatively sloped line with unit gradient, but there is

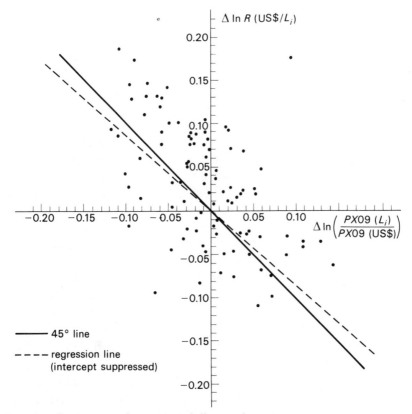

Figure 4   Percentage changes in dollar exchange rates against percentage changes in export prices relative to US export prices.

significant scatter or variance about the line. It does not hold perfectly, or even nearly perfectly. The deviations are generous. Several countries' results over the period 1971–80 are plotted in a time series of cross-sections. There is good support for a law of economics here, but it is only a tendency, subject to error variance.

To a large extent, the economic laws considered up to this point have been time-honored propositions, developed mainly in the nineteenth century. Let us turn now to some twentieth century research into laws of economics.

The modern theory of portfolio analysis goes in many intricate directions, some dictated by institutional structures in financial or credit markets and some by developments in the theory of risk. But, at the core, nearly all the results are derived from a single proposition: "Don't put all your eggs in one basket."[8] The proposition of spreading risk by diversifying portfolio composition is a well-known one, which has been handed down from one generation of investors (scholarly investigators) to another. A theorem concludes that, if the variance of a portfolio's net returns is to be minimized subject to achieving a given average rate of return, the best investment policy is to diversify holdings. By the same token, the maximization of average return, subject to a given variance, will lead to the same result. This is a normative rule, and it is generally observed that there is diversification, but individuals may ignore it. The lucky ones will do well, but the unfortunate ones will lose a great deal by guessing wrong on a concentrated portfolio. Investment advice is usually to diversify; so we can find it prevalent in practice, but this is hard to show or substantiate empirically. It is the perceived widespread acceptance that leads me to classify it as a law of economics.

Harold Hotelling, who contributed fundamentally to several fields, had his successes in economics. He established a law on the exploitation of exhaustible natural resources, and these issues have come to the fore in connection with the analysis of energy problems after 1973. Hotelling's principle is that natural resources should be exploited at rates that tend to equalize the rate of return on all assets together, both exhaustible and other assets, mainly those traded regularly in financial and commodity markets.

---

[8] D. H. Leavens, "Diversification of Investments," *Trusts and Estates* (May 1945).

Hotelling's principle should be looked at as long-run tendency, much as I have looked at PPP above; it should not hold tightly in every short-run situation. It should hold on average, across assets and markets.

Attempts at statistical verification of Hotelling's principle have not been significantly successful at this time; so we are not able now to cite it as a law of economics, but the chances are good that it will be established, as an intermediate- to long-term tendency.

Just as Harold Hotelling spanned many disciplines and made highly original contributions to several, so did John von Neumann, during the productive era of the 1920s–1950s. Although we shall remember von Neumann for many insightful contributions to economics, we ought to remember him most for his important contribution to growth theory in his celebrated paper on intersectoral growth and expansion.[9] Given the usual restrictive assumptions about models of general equilibrium, von Neumann found that the real growth rate of a dynamic economy should equal the real interest rate in long-run equilibrium.

A particularly strict and unusual assumption of the von Neumann model was that workers consume all their income and save nothing. Correspondingly, entrepreneurs save all their income and spend nothing on consumption from their current receipts. Michio Morishima and others relaxed this assumption and established that the real rate of interest should equal the real growth rate divided by the entrepreneurs' marginal savings coefficient. The latter coefficient should be near one, if less than one, and this is seen to be only a minor modification.

It may seem like a very abstruse bit of theorizing, with results that are useful only in theoretical discussion, yet a topical issue of the day is: how long can real interest rates continue to prevail in the face of slow growth (recession) in the real economy? If we look at the disparity between recent real interest rates of some 7 or 8 percent and a negative or near zero growth rate, it is relevant to question whether this state of affairs can prevail for long. The von Neumann result, interpreted as a fundamental economic law, suggests that nominal and real interest rates must eventually (soon) come down from their elevated position and fall into line

---

[9] J. von Neumann, "A Model of General Economic Equilibrium," *Review of Economic Studies* 13 (1945–46): 1–9.

with real growth of the economy. The inflation rate has recently fallen. The prevailing rate is different when computed from different price indexes, but let us say that the underlying inflation rate is about 5 percent. A representative rate in 1981 would be a Treasury bill rate of about 13 percent. This would make the real interest rate 8 percent. When the economy starts to grow, it could sustain a value just below the former trend rate of 4 percent. Let us say that 3 percent would be maintainable. To bring the real interest rate down from 8 percent to about 3 percent would require a reduction in the *nominal* interest rate assuming that the inflation rate will not be further reduced. This is the way that the laws of economic growth can be applied to the analysis of medium-term prospects for the economy. In the short run, the growth rate and real interest rate can diverge, but not for long – say, not more than two or three years; so eventually, I look for easier monetary policy. To say that balance between the real interest and growth rates is to be attained does not indicate how it will be done. It may happen through policy changes, behavioral decision, or a combination of both. Many plausible scenarios can be developed.

In the post-World War II period, with the implementation of the Keynesian system of thought as the mainstream model of macroeconomic reasoning and policy implementation, there was a companion analysis, known as the Phillips curve, to explain inflationary phenomena. In his original contribution, A. W. Phillips established a relationship between nominal wage changes and unemployment. I believe that, as properly stated in the spirit of Phillip's original investigation, this is a sound proposition, although it is in need of elaboration to take account of the dynamics of labor market developments, changing demographic structure, and price change. In these added dimensions, a law of economics prevails. In its relatively brief existence, it has never, in this sense, broken down. It is my opinion that the stagflation of the past decade or so, where we have had simultaneously inflation and high unemployment, did not refute the existence of the Phillips curve, although many economists claimed that it did. I do not mean to go into all the subtle and technical details of the difference between a Phillips curve relationship (between wage changes and unemployment) and a trade-off relationship (between inflation and unemployment), but they are quite different, according to my analysis, and I would claim that we are now witnessing the workings of the Phillips curve relationship on a very broad scale. At present high levels of unemployment, the bargaining power of labor is weakened to such an extent that wage cuts, wage pauses, or wage moderation are the rule in labor market developments. As a law of economics, the Phillips curve is working out just as it should be expected to perform and is a very significant development in contributing to the present lessening of inflationary pressure, through a wage price linkage — namely, productivity.

During the 1950s and early 1960s, when the Phillips curve was just being discussed by economists, Arthur Okun noted that the macroeconomic statistics conformed to a close relationship between unemployment and GNP. An increase of one percentage point in unemployment was associated with a decrease of three percentage points in GNP. His colleagues were so impressed by the strength of this relationship that it came to be called Okun's law. But the three-to-one relationship broke down in the 1970s, when productivity increases came to a halt and there was a surge in the labor force. Extremely simple relationships, particularly bivariate correlations, often look "impressive" for a relatively brief span of time and then break down, just when the investigator convinces himself that he has found a basic law and starts to apply it in the policy process. Economics is like that. Replication, statistical significance, and relative frequency of correct forecast provide exacting batteries of tests that are difficult to pass. To qualify as an economic law, one must ultimately establish more than a decade or two of high correlation. Okun's law is an interesting item of curiosity, but it is not a fundamental economic law, any more than the two-to-one ratio between black and white unemployment rates, which has roughly prevailed in the United States for many years.

Finally, I come to the laws of the business cycle. In this field, there may be many doctrines about duration, amplitude, lead–lag patterns, and other characteristics, but the proposition that I find most fascinating is the "law of the sinusoidal limit." Due independently to R. Frisch, G. Yule, and E. Slutsky, this is a mathematical result that shows how iterated averaging (smoothing) of an erratic time series transforms it into a sine wave. Frisch was the most astute in seeing how this probability process relates to dynamic economic life, but the greatest meaning has been given to the business cycle content of the idea by Irma and Frank Adelman, who showed how stochastic simulation of macroeconometric models produced regular maintained cycles, where only severely damped oscillations existed in a deterministic mode.[10] Subsequent studies have extended, replicated, and verified the Adelmans' findings. This line of reasoning provides statistical and analytical evidence of the existence of the business cycle; it makes the cycle system-free and an aspect of the dynamic–stochastic nature of economic life. It also provides convincing evidence of the existence and explanation of the business cycle as a fundamental law of economic dynamics, just at a time when some economists thought that they had laid the cycle to rest – the fine-tuners of the 1960s and others felt that they were about to do so, as, more recently, the supply-siders and other exponents of "Reaganomics" have done.

In the 1960s, the view of the conquering of the cycle prompted the Committee on Economic Stability of the Social Science Research Council to convene an international meeting under the rubric "Is the Business Cycle Obsolete?" Fortunately, the participants found the cycle very much alive (though weakened in amplitude) just prior to the recurrence of a fresh downturn, in 1969. The absence of a cycle for nine years during the 1960s was a short-run statistical event that prompted the premature feeling of having abolished the cycle.

Two upper turning points in the next decade and two more already in the 1980s in the United States have made us keenly aware of the presence of the business cycle and have even revived discussion of a recurrence of a major depression, which we have not seen for about half a century.

But the importance of the laws of economics is not easily learned. On more than one public occasion, I have pointed out to senior members of the administration's economic team that they planned a five-year expansion of the economy in 1981 without allowance for the existence of a recession in normal cyclical fashion. To my amazement, they replied that they would, by their policies, obliterate the business cycle. Woe to the political economist who

---

[10] I. Adelman and F. Adelman, "The Dynamic Properties of the Klein–Goldberger Model," *Econometrica* 27 (1959): 596–625.

thinks that he can defy the laws of economics, for it is the onset of the 1981 recession that caused their program to unravel. Has not the same thing been happening to our British colleagues? The world recession demonstrated the same lesson for Poland and other borrowers.

Some Qualitative Laws

For the most part, I have been discussing quantitative, or numerical, laws of economics – labor's share, the income elasticity of food consumption, the distribution of income, equality of real interest and growth rates. But I have also mentioned some very general laws, such as the law of supply and demand. Some economists would eschew attempts at careful measurement and related policy recommendations based on statistical estimates of the laws of economics. They prefer to state the laws in qualitative or directional terms, relying on the unseen hand of the free market process to give guidance to the economy.

In discussion of the present fashions in supply side economics, interpreted as responses to large-scale tax cuts, it has been noted that the proponents of SSE could point to logical arguments in support of the directions of effect on which they were relying. I would agree that "their signs are right," but are the effects big enough and fast enough to make their recommendations work as expected? Unfortunately for the economic health of our nation, I fear that reliance on qualitative laws is inadequate in this case and that the effects are too small and too slow to achieve the desired objectives.

At a conference on supply side economics, Milton Friedman declared that it was not particularly a matter of the specialized concepts of SSE, but simply one of "good" economics. "Good" economics would tell us that demand curves slope downwards (respond negatively to price) and that supply curves slope upwards (respond positively to price). Armed with these two qualitative laws, economists could recommend sensible policies. There is a great deal of merit to this point of view, even though it did not work out as planned during 1981–82.

High energy prices eventually induced conservation and general restriction of demand, so that a significant contribution has been made to the lessening of the overriding importance of energy for the functioning of the economy, especially for the reduction of imports.

When the dollar was depreciated during 1977–79, people were very impatient in wanting to see an improvement in the current account balance of the United States. In the early stages of the currency depreciation, we were the victims of the J-curve effect. The relevant international balances moved in a perverse direction because of lags and incomplete pass-throughs of exchange rate changes, but eventually the laws of economics showed through, and the current account responded positively, possibly exaggerating the movement toward surplus and a stronger dollar.

As another example of negatively sloped demand functions, we should consider the response of demand for houses, cars, and capital goods in the face of high interest rates during 1980–82. In an expected way, demand fell markedly and the high rates helped to generate a recession. In these three examples – energy, trade, and durable goods – demand was sensitive to price. As prices rose, demand fell; as prices fell, demand rose. The expected effects occurred in all cases.

Consider now the other side of the qualitative proposition; supply responds positively to price. In this respect, high energy prices induced more drilling and exploration for energy. It also got some projects on synthetics under way. Supplies were significantly increased, as expected.

According to SSE, lower tax rates make after-tax rewards (wages and interest) more attractive. There should be more effort and more savings. We cannot yet see these two things, but they could appear after some delay.

But Milton Friedman neglected to point out that supply curves do not always slope upwards. In economics, there is a law of the backward-bending supply curve of labor. If wage rates are sufficiently high, people may supply less effort, because it is easier for them to meet spending targets, and they may enjoy leisure a great deal. If taxes are cut too far, we may find, in a qualitative sense, a reversal of the shape of the supply curve of effort. This may be one reason why the econometric estimates of labor supply are so pessimistic about the strength of the effect in the interests of SSE.

Summary and Conclusion

There *are* laws of economics. The degree of uncertainty shown by the noise component is not always appreciated by the outsider. If, for some reason or another, people have been led to expect too much from an economic analysis of a problem, they may conclude that there are no laws of economics, or that economists are not properly interpreting them. A realistic understanding of what some typical laws of economics are and the degree of uncertainty that must be involved in drawing conclusions from them should indicate that important non-trivial laws exist and that they can be used to good advantage, even if not to the satisfaction of all.

It is not easy to establish laws of economics, and it is especially dangerous to draw strong conclusions or to base important decisions on apparent correlations, especially in simple bivariate relationships that are discerned in small samples or other sources of limited evidence. Many of these apparent laws break down on embarrassing occasions.

The laws of economics will rarely be sharp enough to allow us to make correct judgments 95 percent of the time within narrow quantitative limits (say plus or minus 5 percent). Economic assessments must be placed within much wider error bands; otherwise our conclusions will be so general as to be non-operational or even empty. Realistic targets for the validity of economic judgments should perhaps be to aim for correctness two-thirds of the time, with precision bands of plus or minus 10 percent.

8 Conclusion

The introduction of the facile concept "supply side economics" seemed to provide new insights that would quickly resolve some of our most pressing problems, but the difficulties are deep-seated and not likely to be dealt with so easily. Understanding this catchy phrase and its relation to the more familiar "demand side economics" in the field of aggregative analysis is the subject matter of this volume.

An answer to the question "What is supply side economics?" cannot be given in a single sentence or paragraph. In fact, three chapters have been used in order to go into the matter in some detail, covering the general meaning, the associated policies, and the outline of the formal theoretical system.

It is not useful to look at either the demand side or the supply side by itself. They are obviously intertwined, as in the "law of supply and demand," and my aim is to show how they fit together. First, let it be said that the popular use of the term "supply side economics" is included in the broader, more scientific sense that is being used here. The popular version considers supply side economics to be synonymous with tax changes that are thought to be closely associated with incentives – incentives to save and incentives to provide effort in jobs. Tax considerations tend to be political, and it is unfortunate that the concept of supply side economics is being considered principally from the viewpoint of its role in the contemporary policy debate; it ought to be considered more broadly from the viewpoint of its role in economic analysis.

In terms of the policy debate, demand management does have a role to play and should not be cast aside. The issue is not to roll back reliance on demand management, but to recognize its limitations. It is necessary but not sufficient, and many supply side policies will have to be introduced if the problem of stagflation is to be overcome. But the more important distinction is not between demand side and supply side policies; it is between *aggregative* and *structural* policies. The problems of the day that cannot be attacked by macro-demand management alone are policies associated with

shortfalls of basic resources
stockpile management
age and other demographic composition of unemployment
environmental protection – atmosphere, stream, solid waste
energy
food
productivity improvement
export competitiveness.

Progress in dealing with these problems will hardly be affected by macro-policies of either sort, whether on the demand or the supply side. This means that economic policy cannot be conducted solely along the lines of shifts in overall tax rates, variations in expenditure totals, control of monetary aggregates, or general changes in tariffs. Policy will have to be more specific. *Structural* policies will be those aimed at particular age groups, particular kinds of raw material availability, particular incursions on the environment, provision of energy in particular forms, and the improvement of cost efficiency in selected lines. A great deal of economic policy along these lines falls under the heading of "industrial policy."

Suggestions can be made about specific structural policies, but it is premature to spell out the details. First, the general principle about proceeding in this way needs to be understood and accepted. Specific policies can then be put into place with the necessary back-drop of legality and bureaucratic procedures.

A *theory* must underlie this view of the economy – one that can be used for the sound formation and generation of applied research. The theory can be outlined in the form of the Keynes–Leontief Model. Aggregate demand for a few macro-categories, the formation of factor incomes, and the determination of market indicators (prices, wage rates, interest rates) follow the well-known Keynesian model-building lines. The production technology, productivity trends, and inter-industry flows are generated by a version of the Leontief system – a version in which input–output coefficients are treated as variables, dependent on shifts in relative prices. This is a large-scale dynamic system. It is also non-linear and stochastic. This system is capable of displaying the policy instruments of aggregative demand management and structural supply side policy. This means that tax rates, public expenditure totals, monetary reserve variables, age classes of population groups, specific industry or sector activity levels, the term structure of interest rates, foreign exchange rates, tariff duties, and many other specific instruments must be isolated in the system. The Wharton Annual Model has these various properties. It can be used as a theoretical back-drop for medium-range policies and can be combined with a more aggregative quarterly model for detailed, short-run policy analysis.

Given the understanding of the concepts and a theoretical model for analysis, does there exist a set of policies that can, in fact, overcome the problem of stagflation? Policies can be recommended, in the form of a total program, but they have never been tried all together. It is expected that they will work, given a fair period of gestation – about three or four years. In a positive vein, the policies consist of

(i) tax-based investment stimuli, with some differentiation by sector

(ii) on-the-job private sector training schemes for workers, especially youth

(iii) inflation monitoring of the regulatory process

(iv) industrial policy based on a bold approach of trying to "pick the winners"

(v) export promotion

(vi) environmental protection

(vii) an energy program based on coal, fuels, and other oil substitutes, with a stockpiling policy

(viii) raw materials stockpiling

(ix) youth differential in minimum wages

(x) tax stimuli for venture capital, as in rollover proposals

(xi) policies for the promotion of savings, such as portability of pensions

(xii) increased support for R & D and basic research.

A broad-based incomes policy should be held in reserve in case of need — in other words, in case these other programs do not fully deal with inflationary pressures.

The economic environment in which these policies are to be implemented, both domestically and internationally, is one that has changed markedly from recent historical experience. The world grew quickly during the 1950s and 1960s. There was turbulence and cyclical fluctuation during the 1970s, resulting in the present state of stagflation. There may be as many as 35 million people unemployed in the OECD countries in a year or two, coincident with higher rates of inflation than occurred in the 1950s and 1960s. In some instances, the inflation rate may exceed 10 percent, and it is rarely expected to fall to less than 5 percent. Outside the industrial world, good statistics of unemployment and inflation are more difficult to obtain. The concepts are also more complicated in the developing and centrally planned economies, yet these two groupings of countries are also beset with some form of inflationary pressure and slow growth prospects.

A popular forecast projects world growth at about one percent less than in the 1950s and 1960s, together with higher inflation rates. Productivity, which slowed down during the 1970s, should start to regain some of its former expansiveness, but not up to the growth rates of the 1960s. World trade should be on a slower path, growing at about 5 or 6 percent annually. This offers a poor prospect for the oil-importing developing countries, who depend on vigorous expansion of trade in order to capture a share for themselves that will provide some export-led growth.

Thus, the economic environment will be conducive to stagflation, and it will require vigorous application of the program listed above to break out of this bind. There *is* a more optimistic scenario and prospect, but it will not be achieved through the application of conventional policies, especially purely macro-policies.

In medium-term projections, it is customary to establish a baseline scenario that has normal inputs — normal weather, no military disturbance, no natural disasters, no unusual energy interruptions. Our experience has been that decade-long periods are never completely normal. The Korean War and the closing of the Suez Canal jolted the 1950s; in the 1960s, the Vietnam War was the main disturbance; the 1970s witnessed massive harvest failures in the USSR, an oil embargo, OPEC pricing, and the Iranian revolution.

We do not know where or when a mid-decade disturbance will occur during the 1980s, but it is possible to try to allow for some contingencies by simulating alternative cases that have some of the characteristics of past disturbances. Some hypothetical oil shocks based on supply interruptions with large price increases have been simulated for the 1980s. These scenarios are indexed to OECD export price inflation and real growth. The base case is close to what is known as the OPEC indexation formula for oil pricing.

Not all price jumps give a worse outcome than that provided by the baseline case, but if the interruption is such that crude oil prices are temporarily driven far above the indexed increase and then recede to the same end point, as in the baseline case, there would be a net loss in world production and overall activity. In the fullest sense of interpretation of supply side economics, these scenarios with mid-decade disturbances show what that branch of our subject is all about.

We have not, in this volume, introduced new branches of economics or novel methods of analysis. What we have tried to do is to gather together known branches of our subject and known techniques in order to use them in as complete a way as possible, with the greatest degree of interaction that we have been able to manage, to examine contemporary and future economic problems of the world.

Appendix: The Formal Structure of Supply Side Models

There are essentially two ways of studying industrial sectors of an economy from an econometric point of view. One approach integrates the detailed industrial composition of an economy directly into a model of the economy as a whole. This is the Walrasian approach. Another methodology is to build a separate (satellite) model of a sector and estimate specific linkage relations to tie this model to an overall model of the economy. And we shall see that possible combinations of these two approaches can also be implemented.

Input–output, or inter-industry, analysis is a standard method of integrating separate industrial output variables in a nationally consistent way. This approach, in its standard form, does not simultaneously determine the macro-components of final demand and value added. Much less does it determine interest rates, prices, wage rates, financial flows, inventory investment, and other general economy variables. It usually proceeds with a fixed coefficient matrix and does not relate the changing input–output structure to varying market conditions.

The well-known formula of input–output (I–O) analysis is

$$(I - A)X = F$$

where A = matrix of I–O coefficients

$$a_{ij} = X_{ij}/X_j$$

X = vector of gross outputs
F = vector of final demands.

137

In its simplest form, this system is defined for a fixed A matrix, real (constant-price) X, real F. It is not a closed system, in that F must be known in advance in order to derive a solution for X:

$$X = (I - A)^{-1} F.$$

It is the purpose of this presentation to show how a macro-model to explain F can be introduced, how market variables can be simultaneously introduced, how the A matrix can be made variable, and how several variables for each industrial sector can be introduced.

In order to appreciate the modeling problem fully, it is instructive to examine the accounting structure. Consider the *current-price* diagram in Figure A1. In the main $(N \times N)$ square array, the inter-industry deliveries of output from any sector i to any sector j are tabulated. The typical element is X_{ij}; this is the numerator of a conventional I–O coefficient if it is defined in current prices.

The right-hand rectangular group is the matrix of deliveries to final demand. In this case, final demand is split into categories, C (consumption), I (investment), G (government expenditures), E (exports), and M (imports – entered negatively). The column sums of this rectangular matrix give a row of GNP account entries. The row sum is, in fact, GNP:

$$C + I + G + E - M = GNP.$$

The disaggregation of F into columns is not unique; it is only illustrative. In detailed model-building, it should be much more disaggregated. The Wharton model has had more than 40 columns for several (model) generations.

The bottom rectangular group is a matrix of values added by sector. Each column of the entire array gives gross output (X), just as each row also gives gross output. While the row sums are broken up into intermediate and final deliveries, the column sums are broken up into intermediate input and value added. The row sums of the bottom matrix provide a column of national income (or national value added) components:

$$NI = W + IN + PR$$

where W = wages
      IN = interest
      PR = profits.

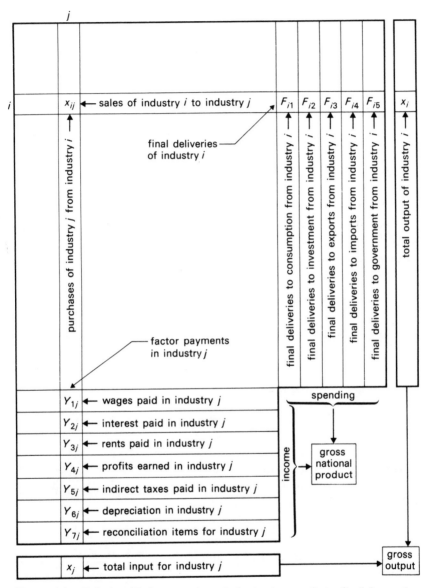

Figure A1 Relationship between inter-industry transactions, final demand, and factor payments

Value added can be split into more disaggregated components covering royalties, rent, types of wages, etc. If indirect taxes and capital consumption allowance are entered positively, while subsidies are entered negatively, we would have the basic GNP identity:

$$NI + IT + CC - SU = GNP.$$

where IT = indirect taxes

CC = capital consumption allowances

SU = subsidies.

Apart from measurement error (statistical discrepancy), these two totals for GNP should be the same, whether measured from F or VA.

Two new matrices will be introduced, one to convert gross output into value added and the other to relate final demand to GNP components. Form the identity

$$VA_j = X_j - \sum_{i=1}^{n} a_{ij}X_j = \left(1 - \sum_{i=1}^{n} a_{ij}\right) X_j.$$

In matrix terms,

$$VA = Y = BX$$

where B is a diagonal matrix with

$$\left(1 - \sum_{i=1}^{n} a_{ij}\right)$$

in the jth diagonal location.

Each entry of the F matrix is to be divided by its column total to form a new matrix C. We then have

$$F = C\mathscr{G}$$

where $\mathscr{G}$ is a vector of GNP components $- C, I, G, E, - M$ in this example.

We can now write

$$(I - A) B^{-1}Y = C\mathscr{G}$$

$$Y = B(I - A)^{-1}C\mathscr{G}.$$

This provides a full linkage between $\mathscr{G}$ and Y, between the GNP and the value added, both disaggregated into their own group of sectors.

Macroeconometric models are designed to generate $\mathscr{G}$ (with its components) and Y (with its components). These are national expenditure and income models. These are current price relationships and, when considered together with physical production relationships, must have properly associated equations for market variables – wage rates, prices, interest rates by sector.

This explains the relationships among elements of $\mathscr{G}$ and Y, with indications about related market variables. It is now in order to deal with variable I–O coefficients a_{ij}. No one argues that the matrix A remains constant through time, but fresh approaches are necessary in order to extend input–output modeling systematically to cover the variation of components of A. This linkage will be developed in relation to the price system; in other words, changes in relative prices will be used as indicators of changes in elements of A.

If the inter-industry flows are measured in current prices, we may write them explicitly as

$$\frac{p_i X_{ij}}{p_j X_j} = \alpha_{ij}.$$

The *conventional* input–output measure would be

$$a_{ij} = \frac{X_{ij}}{X_j} = \alpha_{ij} \left(\frac{p_i}{p_j} \right)^{-1.0}.$$

If the α_{ij} are stable parameters, then a_{ij} ("real" input–output coefficients) vary as relative prices vary (inversely proportional to (p_i/p_j)). Any two inputs would vary according to

$$\frac{X_{ij}}{X_{kj}} = \frac{\alpha_{ij}}{\alpha_{kj}} \left(\frac{p_i}{p_k} \right)^{-1.0}.$$

This result could be derived from an extended Cobb–Douglas production function, where the elasticity of substitution among input pairs is always 1.0, and all intermediate inputs are joint factors in the production function. It is a condition for cost minimization.

A more general formulation is to use the relationship

$$\frac{X_{ij}}{X_{kj}} = \left(\frac{\alpha_{ij}}{\alpha_{kj}}\right)^{\sigma_j} \left(\frac{p_i}{p_k}\right)^{-\sigma_j}.$$

For each industry ($j = 1, 2, \ldots, n$), a CES production function instead of a Cobb–Douglas is used to relate output to the joint collection of intermediate inputs. This introduces one more parameter, σ_j, and relaxes the assumption of unitary elasticity of substitution. The α_{ij} are the distributional parameters of the CES specification.

Since σ_j is assumed, in this specification, to be the same between all input pairs into j, we can use cross-industry or sector variation as well as time variation to estimate σ_j.

There will also be labor and capital variation in every sector; so we might write the whole relationship as

$$\text{Cobb–Douglas} \quad X_j = A_j \sum_{i=1}^{n} X_{ij}^{\alpha_{ij}} L_j^{\alpha_j} K_j^{\beta_j} e^{\gamma_j t}$$

or

$$\text{CES} \quad X_j = A_j \left(\sum_{i=1}^{n} \alpha_{ij} X_{ij}^{-\rho_j}\right)^{-1/\rho_j} L_j^{\alpha_j} K_j^{\beta_j} e^{\gamma_j t}$$

$$\rho_j = \frac{1}{1 + \sigma_j} \qquad \sum_{i=1}^{n} \alpha_{ij} = 1.$$

The production function need not separate into intermediate and original factor input functions in a multiplicative specification. Additive specifications are possible, as well. The important idea is that a general function is used

$$X_j = F_j(X_{ij}, \ldots, X_{nj}, L_j, K_j, t)$$

and the variable I–O coefficients are derived from it, using a cost minimization or profit maximization principle. It is this latter idea that leads us to argue that I–O coefficients will vary as functions of relative price variation.[1]

---

[1] For specific applications, see M. Saito, "An Interindustry Study of Price Formation," *The Review of Economics and Statistics* 53 (February 1971): 11–25; and R. S. Preston, "The Wharton Long Term Model: Input–Output within the Context of a Macro Forecasting Model," *International Economic Review* 16 (February 1975): 3–19.

This is a static analysis and is most suited for equilibrium models. To the extent that the actual economy, from which data are taken, is out of equilibrium, we need a dynamic adjustment process for short-run analysis. This is complicated by the requirement that accounting identities must be satisfied by all data, whether in equilibrium or not.

The treatment of final demand can be consistently implemented within this same framework if complete expenditure systems are used. If consumer demand, for example, can be identified with expenditure categories of the GNP according to sector of origin in the I–O table, we could then use the linear, S-branch, or similar system to estimate all the categories in a way that satisfies budget identities.

Let F_{ic} be the delivery in F from the ith sector to consumer demand. For each i or subgroup $(i, j, k, \ldots)$, we must establish a correspondence with a component of C in the GNP accounts. A linear system would be

$$F_{ic} = a_i p_i + b_i \left(Y - \sum_{j=1}^{n} a_j p_j\right).$$

This would enable one to deal with varying ratios F_{ic}/C in the F matrix in the same way that we propose to do this in the A matrix. A similar analysis would have to be extended to other components of final demand, and an extension to dynamic adjustment would also have to be introduced.[2]

From an indicative point of view, this is the way that generalized inter-industry systems can be modeled on a comprehensive and systematic basis, especially with changing I–O coefficients. Let us now turn to the idea of industrial sector analysis on a satellite model basis.

A model of a sector would be designed to explain such things as

production
factor inputs (intermediate and original)
factor prices (wage rates, interest rates, material prices, energy prices)
output prices

---

[2] For total final demand as a single aggregate over expenditure categories, this has been done by Th. Gamaletsos, "Forecasting Sectoral Final Demand by a Dynamic Generalized Linear Expenditure System," Center of Planning and Economic Research (Athens, 1978). He uses a generalization of the linear expenditure system to estimate a consistent set of final demand equations in the context of an input–output system.

shipments
inventories
profits
costs.

Multiproduct and multifactor processes are possible, as well as stage of process. A typical econometric approach is to write the model as

production function $\quad X_i^s = f_x(K_i, L_i, E_i, M_i)$

factor demand functions $\quad K_i = f_K(p_i, r_i, w_i, q_i, g_i, X_i^s)$

$$L_i = f_L(p_i, r_i, w_i, q_i, g_i, X_i^s)$$

$$E_i = f_E(p_i, r_i, w_i, q_i, g_i, X_i^s)$$

$$M_i = f_M(p_i, r_i, w_i, q_i, g_i, X_i^s)$$

product demand $\quad X_i^D = g(Y, p_i, p_j)$

inventory function $\quad X_i^s - X_i^D = h(\Delta X_i^D, \Delta p_i, S_i)$

factor price equations $\quad r_i = k_r(r)$

$$w_i = k_w(w)$$

$$q_i = k_q(q)$$

$$g_i = k_g(g)$$

output price $\quad \Delta p_i = k_p(X_i^s - X_i^D)$

The production function is a standard relation between output in the ith sector (X_i) and factor inputs $(K_i =$ capital, $L_i =$ labor, $E_i =$ energy, $M_i =$ materials). The factor demand functions would be specified as a result of an optimization process, ending up as functions of output price (p_i), factor input prices $(r_i =$ capital rental, $w_i =$ wage rate, $q_i =$ energy price, and $g_i =$ materials price). Output level is also a variable in the factor demand function.

The demand function for the ith sector's product will be a function of price (p_i), national income level (Y), and price of related goods (p_j). Other, more specific, variables may determine demand for the product. In particular, it may not be an issue of general demand in the economy at large, in which case the suitable activity variable would not be aggregate income (Y) but a more specialized variable such as X_j^D or foreign demand, or aggregate production in the economy instead of aggregate income.

Demand and supply need not, and probably will not, balance in every period. Their discrepancy will be the *change* in inventory stocks. Thus, the equation for $(X^s - X^D)$ is an equation for the flow into or out of stock. Inventory equations are not often very satisfactory, but this one, in the present case, is a very ordinary function, depending on production change (ΔX_i^D) price change (p_i) and carrying costs (S = storage plus interest).

The equations for factor prices are made simple functions of corresponding national prices. There may be some specific variable in any, or all, of these equations, but, generally speaking, sector factor prices will follow national factor prices in the corresponding lines of activity.

Finally, output price is assumed to balance supply and demand in this sector; thus p_i should fluctuate in response to its own inventory changes.

Many refinements and variations, specific to the sector being studied in satellite mode, would in practice be introduced, although the main lines of effect would be as indicated. But market variables (product and factor prices) will largely follow national prices. In addition, national demand factors will probably dominate sector i's product demand.

The output of the total national model will be used, after solution, to serve, as needed, for input into the estimated sector model. It will then be solved for sector variables. These may be used, when appropriate, in the national model. For example, specific intermediate deliveries can be put directly into the I–O system. Other feedback effects can be linked also. Then the large national model is solved again and input for the satellite model is linked into it. This procedure is then iterated until there are no significant changes on successive rounds. Usually, not many iterations – fewer than six – are needed in order to obtain convergence of both models.

Once the inputs, outputs, prices, and other variables generated by the satellite model are obtained, there are a number of transformations and identities that can be used to obtain measures of such concepts as profits and costs. Costs of intermediate inputs $q_i E_i$ and $g_i M_i$ are aggregative components of the column entries of the input–output table for the ith sector. By spreading these aggregates throughout the column, it is possible to allow the satellite model to be used to move the A matrix through time. Of course, types of E and M components can be built into a more detailed satellite model production function and provide more direct information for the input–output matrix. Feedback effects from the satellite can occur in other dimensions, as well. If the demand and output are multiproduct, we can disaggregate into deliveries along the ith row of the I–O matrix. Satellite models can be used to move rows as well as columns of the matrix. Also, feedback can occur for specific prices, wage rates, final demand, or value added components of the whole large model. If the ith sector, for example, is the motor vehicle industry, then direct estimates of the automobile component of C (from the GNP accounts) can be obtained from the satellite model for use in the system as a whole.

For interest in any one sector, the procedure of linking a satellite model to a model of the economy as a whole is straightforward. If there are several satellite models, they may be interrelated among themselves, and this aspect needs to be built into the specification. Also, care must be taken to insure consistency with the system as a whole if the collection of satellites makes up a significant and important part of the total economy.

It is probably not feasible to devote detailed attention to all possible satellite models in a system of fifty or more sectors. A preferred approach is to model almost all sectors uniformly through an input–output system. That is the best single approach, but any small number of strategic sectors can be accommodated in satellite fashion.

Econometric models are powerful and useful, but they do not provide the only approach to sector modeling or the best approach for all problems. The use of programming models opens up an avenue for augmenting the strict econometric method and for adding technological information to mainly economic information in a constructive way. A *linear* program for a sector can be expressed as:

$$p'x = \max$$

subject to

$$c'x \leqslant C$$

$$Tx \leqslant b$$

when p is a column vector of output prices
    c is a column vector of input prices
    x is a column vector of activity levels
    T is a rectangular matrix of technological coefficients
    b is a column vector of material balances constraints
    C is total cost (constraint).

The prices (p, c), optimal (constraint) levels of operation (b), and matrix of coefficients (T) are assumed to be given. The maximization problem can be handled by well-known methods. It is used, however, in a unique way for combination with large-scale models.

From technical information, there are typical programming models for individual industries. Some leading cases are oil refineries, petrochemical plants, steel plants, and electric power stations. For any one of these cases, let us suppose that the details of a linear program are computed for a given price vector.

A pioneer in this development writes:

> This paper explores a new approach to the estimation of a joint production technology. Pseudo data, which are obtained by solving a petrochemical process model for alternative relative prices, are used to estimate a price possibility frontier with 3 inputs and 6 outputs. Unlike traditional data sources, pseudo data are not constrained by historical price variations, technologies, and environmental controls. As an econometric exercise, the approximation of this process model's detailed piecewise linear production surface by a single equation "generalized" functional form, the translog, raises a host of interesting empirical and methodological question.[3]

The linear program, as stated, can be solved for given p, c, C, T, b. By varying p and c in a systematic way, we can obtain solutions to the programming problem for each p, c vector. By appropriately varying prices, it is possible to generate and preserve a large body of statistical data on different observations for cost and production, among other variables. The translog specification would make each factor's cost share a linear function (constrained) of

---

[3] James M. Griffin, "Joint Production Technology: The Case of Petrochemicals," *Econometrica* 46 (2 March 1978): 379–96.

logarithms of input prices. By regression analysis on the pseudo data, the equations for cost shares and total cost can be determined. These cost functions may be used for any satellite or directly related cost figures in updated I-O tables. Either the programming problem can be left fully intact for detailed applications, or it can be used to generate "pseudo" data, to which cost functions will be fit. These cost functions are then used like any other cost functions that serve for determining intermediate outputs or inputs.

Whether it be through a traditional econometric model or a programming system, the results should be similar and placed in the appropriate position in an I-O table for the express purpose of moving the technical coefficients from one time point to the next.

A priori engineering or operational information is used in constructing the linear program. In this way, new technical processes can be introduced and estimated by econometric cost functions even though observational samples of data are not historically available. That is the power of the method for long-range modeling, as in the case of energy systems.

Sector analysis, whether by I-O methods, ordinary econometric models of satellite systems, or by engineering design, is a promising and growing field of model-building activity. All methods together complement one another, and no single approach should be relied upon exclusively.

The Author's Publications

Books

The Keynesian Revolution (New York: Macmillan, 1947), 2nd ed. 1966.
Economic Fluctuations in the United States, 1921–1941 (New York: Wiley, 1950).
A Textbook of Econometrics (Evanston, Ill.: Row, Peterson, and Co., 1953); 2nd ed. (Englewood Cliffs, New Jersey: Prentice-Hall, 1974).
Contributions of Survey Methods to Economics (with G. Katona, J. Lansing, and J. Morgan) (New York: Columbia University Press, 1954).
An Econometric Model of the United States, 1929–1952 (with A. S. Goldberger) (Amsterdam: North-Holland, 1955).
An Econometric Model of the United Kingdom (with R. J. Ball, A. Hazlewood, and P. Vandome) (Oxford: Basil Blackwell, 1961).
An Introduction to Econometrics (Englewood Cliffs, New Jersey: Prentice-Hall, 1962).
Readings in Business Cycles, ed. with R. A. Gordon, for the American Economic Association (Homewood, Ill.: Richard D. Irwin, 1965).
The Brookings Quarterly Econometric Model of the United States, ed. with J. Duesenberry, G. Fromm, and E. Kuh (Chicago: Rand McNally, 1965).
The Wharton Index of Capacity Utilization (with R. Summers) (Philadelphia: Wharton School of Finance and Commerce, 1967).
The Wharton Econometric Forecasting Model (with M. K. Evans) (Philadelphia: Wharton School of Finance and Commerce, 1967); 2nd enlarged ed., 1968.
Economic Growth: The Japanese Experience Since the Meiji Era, ed. with K. Ohkawa (Homewood, Ill.: Richard D. Irwin, 1968).
The Brookings Model: Some Further Results, ed. with J. Duesenberry, G. Fromm, and E. Kuh (Chicago: Rand McNally, 1969).

149

An Essay on the Theory of Economic Prediction (Helsinki: Yrjö Jahnsson Foundation, 1969); 2nd enlarged ed. (Chicago: Markham, 1971).

Econometric Gaming: A Kit for Computer Analysis of Macroeconomic Models, with M. K. Evans and M. Hartley (New York: Macmillan Co., 1969).

Essays in Industrial Econometrics, ed. in 3 vols (Philadelphia: Wharton School of Finance and Commerce, 1969).

The Brookings Model: Perspective and Recent Developments, ed. with Gary Fromm (Amsterdam: North-Holland, 1975).

Econometric Model Performance, ed. with E. Burmeister (Philadelphia: University of Pennsylvania Press, 1976).

An Introduction to Econometric Forecasting and Forecasting Models (with R. M. Young) (Lexington, Mass.: D. C. Heath, Lexington Books, 1980).

Quantitative Economics and Development: Essays in Memory of Ta-Chung Liu, ed. with M. Nerlove and S. C. Tsiang (New York: Academic Press, 1980).

Econometric Models as Guides for Decision Making (New York: The Free Press, 1981), The Charles C. Moskowitz Memorial Lecture Series.

Articles

"Pitfalls in the Statistical Determination of the Investment Schedule," *Econometrica*, Vol. 11, July–October, 1943, 246–58.

"The Statistical Determination of the Investment Schedule: A Reply," *Econometrica*, Vol. 12, January 1944, 91–2.

"The Cost of a 'Beveridge Plan' in the United States," *Quarterly Journal of Economics*, Vol. LVIII, May 1944, 423–37.

"Macroeconomics and the Theory of Rational Behavior," *Econometrica*, Vol. 14, April 1946, 93–108.

"Dispersal of Cities and Industries," with J. Marschak and E. Teller, *Bulletin of the Atomic Scientists*, Vol. 1, 13–15, 20.

"A Post-Mortem on Transition Predictions of National Product," *Journal of Political Economy*, Vol. LIV, August 1946, 289–308.

"Remarks on the Theory of Aggregation," *Econometrica*, Vol. 14, October 1946, 303–12.

"The Use of Econometric Models as a Guide to Economic Policy," *Econometrica*, Vol. 15, April 1947, 111–51.

"Theories of Effective Demand and Employment," *Journal of Political Economy*, Vol. LV, April 1947, 108–31.

"Notes on the Theory of Investment," *Kyklos*, 1948, Vol. 2, 97–117.

"Planned Economy in Norway," *American Economic Review*, Vol. XXXVIII, December 1948, 795–814.

"Economic Planning – Western European Style," *Statsøkonomisk Tidsskrift*, Vols. 3–4, 1948, 97–124.

"A Constant-Utility Index of the Cost of Living," with H. Rubin, *Review of Economic Studies*, Vol. XV (2) 1947-48, 84-7.

"A Scheme of International Compensation," *Econometrica*, Vol. 17, April 1949, 145-59.

"Stock and Flow Analysis in Economics," *Econometrica*, Vol. 18, July 1950, 236-41, 246.

"The Dynamics of Price Flexibility: A Comment," *American Economic Review*, Vol. XL, September 1950, 605-9.

"The Life of John Maynard Keynes," *Journal of Political Economy*, Vol. LIX, October 1951, 443-51.

"Estimating Patterns of Savings Behavior from Sample Survey Data," *Econometrica*, Vol. 19, October 1951, 438-54.

"Studies in Investment Behavior," *Conference on Business Cycles*, National Bureau of Economic Research, New York, 1951, 233-303.

"Results of Alternative Statistical Treatments of Sample Survey Data," with J. N. Morgan, *Journal of the American Statistical Association*, Vol. 46 (December 1951), 442-60.

"Assets, Debts, and Economic Behavior," *Studies in Income and Wealth*, Vol. 14 (National Bureau of Economic Research, New York, 1951), 197-227.

"Psychological Data in Business Cycle Research," with G. Katona, *American Journal of Economics and Sociology*, Vol. 12, October 1952, 11-22.

"On the Interpretation of Professor Leontief's System," *Review of Economic Studies*, Vol. XX, 1952-53, 131-6.

"National Income and Product, 1929-50," *American Economic Review*, Vol. XLIII, March 1953, 117-32.

"Savings Concepts and Data: The Needs of Economic Analysis and Policy," *Savings in the Modern Economy*, ed. W. W. Heller, F. M. Boddy, and C. L. Nelson (Minneapolis: University of Minnesota Press, 1953), 104-7.

"Negro-White Savings Differentials and the Consumption Function Problem," with H. W. Mooney, *Econometrica*, Vol. XXI, 1953, 425-56.

"The Estimation of Disposable Income by Distributive Shares," with Lenore Frane, *Review of Economics and Statistics*, Vol. XXXV, November 1953, 333-7.

"A 'Mild Down Turn' in American Trade," with A. S. Goldberger, *Manchester Guardian Weekly*, January 7, 1954, 3.

"Statistical Studies of Unincorporated Business," with J. Margolis, *Review of Economics and Statistics*, Vol. XXXVI, February 1954, 33-46.

"Savings and the Propensity to Consume," *Determining the Business Outlook*, ed. H. Prochnow (New York: Harper and Bros., 1954), 109-25.

"A Quarterly Model of the United States Economy," with H. Barger, *Journal of the American Statistical Association*, Vol. 49, September 1954, 413-37.

"Empirical Foundations of Keynesian Economics," *Post Keynesian Economics*, ed. K. K. Kurihara (New Brunswick: Rutgers University Press, 1954).

"The Contribution of Mathematics in Economics," *Review of Economics and Statistics*, Vol. XXXVI, November 1954, 359-61.

"The U.S. Economy in 1955," *Manchester Guardian*, January 3, 1955.

"British and American Consumers – A Comparison of Their Situations and Finances," *The Bankers Magazine*, March 1955, 241-6.

"The Savings Survey 1953 – Response Rates and Reliability of Data," with T. P. Hill and K. H. Straw, *Bulletin of the Oxford University Institute of Statistics*, Vol. 17, 1955, 91-126.

"Major Consumer Expenditures and Ownership of Durable Goods," *Bulletin of the Oxford University Institute of Statistics*, Vol. 17, 1955, 387-414.

"Decisions to Purchase Consumer Durable Goods," with J. B. Lansing, *Journal of Marketing*, Vol. XX, 1955, 109-32.

"Statistical Testing of Business Cycle Theory: The Econometric Method," *The Business Cycle in the Post-War World*, ed. E. Lundberg (London: Macmillan, 1955).

"On the Interpretation of Theil's Method of Estimating Economic Relationships," *Metroeconomica*, Vol. VII, December 1955, 147-53.

"Insulation of the Modern Economy," *The Banker's Magazine*, January 1956, 1-5.

"The Practicability of an Expenditure Tax in the Light of the Oxford Savings Survey," *The Banker's Magazine*, March 1956, 235-9.

"Personal Savings and the Budget," *The Banker's Magazine*, June 1956, 485-9.

"Econometric Models and the Evidence of Time Series Analysis," *The Manchester School*, Vol. XXIV, May 1956, 197-201.

"Patterns of Savings – The Surveys of 1953 and 1954," *Bulletin of the Oxford University Institute of Statistics*, Vol. 17, 1955, 173-214.

"Savings and Finances of the Upper Income Classes," with K. H. Straw and P. Vandome, *Bulletin of the Oxford University Institute of Statistics*, Vol. 18, 1956, 293-319.

"Quelques Aspects Empiriques du Modele de Cycle Economique de Kaldor," *Les Modeles dynamiques en econometrie* (Paris: Centre National de la Recherche Scientifique, 1956).

"The Scope and Limitations of Econometrics," *Applied Statistics*, Vol. VI, 1957, 1-18.

"A Note on 'Middle-Range' Formulation," *Common Frontiers of the Social Sciences*, ed. M. Komarovsky (Glencoe, Ill.: Free Press, 1957), 383-91.

"The Interpretation of Leontief's System – A Reply," *Review of Economic Studies*, Vol. XXXV (1), 1956-57, 69-70.

"Sampling Errors in the Savings Surveys," with Peter Vandome, *Bulletin of the Oxford University Institute of Statistics*, Vol. 19, 1957, 85-105.

"The Significance of Income Variability on Saving Behavior," with N. Liviatan, *Bulletin of the Oxford University Institute of Statistics*, Vol. 19, 1957, 151-60.

"Trade of the United Kingdom and the Sterling Area in Two American Recessions," with R. J. Ball and A. Hazlewood, *The Banker's Magazine*, Vol. CLXXXV, 1957, 426-31.

"The British Propensity to Save," *Journal of the Royal Statistical Society*, Series A (general), Vol. 121, 1958, 60-96.

"The Friedman-Becker Illusion," *Journal of Political Economy*, Vol. LXVI, 1958, 539-45.

"Econometric and Sample Survey Methods of Forecasting," *Business Forecasting*, Pub. No. 3 of the Market Research Society (London, 1958), 9-18.

"Econometric Forecasts for 1959," with R. J. Ball and A. Hazlewood, *Bulletin of the Oxford University Institute of Statistics*, Vol. 21, 1959, 3-16.

"The Estimation of Distributed Lags," *Econometrica*, Vol. 26, October 1958, 553-65.

"Some Econometrics of the Determination of Absolute Prices and Wages," with R. J. Ball, *Economic Journal*, Vol. LXIX, September 1959, 465-82.

"Economic Forecasting," *Kyklos*, Vol. XII, 1959, Fasc. 4, 650-7.

"The American Balance-of-Payments Problem," *The Banker's Magazine*, April 1960, 299-305.

"Some Theoretical Issues in the Measurement of Capacity," *Econometrica*, Vol. 28, April 1960, 272-86.

"The Efficiency of Estimation in Econometric Models," *Essays in Economics and Econometrics*, ed. R. W. Pfouts (Chapel Hill: University of North Carolina Press, 1960), 216-32.

"Single Equation vs. Equation System Methods of Estimation in Econometrics," *Econometrica*, Vol. 28, October 1960, 866-71.

"Entrepreneurial Saving," *Proceedings of the Conference on Income and Saving*, Vol. II, ed. I. Friend and R. Jones (Philadelphia: University of Pennsylvania Press, 1960), 297-335.

"Re-Estimation of the Econometric Model of the U.K. and Forecasts for 1961," with A. Hazlewood and P. Vandome, *Bulletin of the Oxford University Institute of Statistics*, Vol. 23, 1961, 23-40.

"Some Econometrics of Growth: Great Ratios of Economics," with R. F. Kosobud, *The Quarterly Journal of Economics*, Vol. LXXV, 1961, 173-98.

"A Model of Japanese Economic Growth, 1878-1937," *Econometrica*, Vol. 29, July 1961, 277-92.

"Measuring Soviet Industrial Growth," *Bulletin of the Oxford University Institute of Statistics*, Vol. 20, 1958, 373-7.

"An Econometric Analysis of the Postwar Relationship between Inventory Fluctuations and Changes in Aggregate Economic Activity," with J. Popkin, *Inventory Fluctuations and Economic Stabilization*, Part III, Joint Economic Committee, US Congress, Washington, USGPO, 1961, 69-89.

"The Measurement of Industrial Capacity," Hearings Before the Sub-Committee on Economic Statistics, JEC 87th Congress, 2nd Session, May 1962, 53-9.

"Singularity in the Equation Systems of Econometrics: Some Aspects of the Problem of Multicollinearity," with M. Nakamura, *International Economic Review*, III, September 1962, 274-99.

"An Econometric Model of Japan, 1930-59," with Y. Shinkai, *International Economic Review*, IV, January 1963, 1-29.

"A Postwar Quarterly Model: Description and Applications," *Models of Income Determination, Studies in Income and Wealth*, Vol. 28 (Princeton University Press, 1964), 11-36.

"Empirical Aspects of the Trade-Offs Among Three Goals: High Level Employment, Price Stability and Economic Growth," with R. G. Bodkin, *Inflation, Growth and Employment*, Commission on Money and Credit (New York: Prentice-Hall, 1964), 367–428.

"A Quarterly Econometric Model of Japan, 1952–1959," with S. Ichimura, S. Koizumi, K. Sato and Y. Shinkai, *Osaka Economic Papers*, Vol. XXII, March 1964, 19–44.

"Economics as a Behavioral Science," *The Behavioral Sciences: Problems and Prospects* (Institute of Behavioral Science, University of Colorado, August 1964), 21–26.

"The Social Science Research Council Econometric Model of the United States," *Colston Papers*, Vol. XVI (University of Bristol, 1964), 129–68.

"The Keynesian Revolution Revisited," *Economic Studies Quarterly*, XV, November 1964, 1–24.

"The Role of Econometrics in Socialist Economics," *Problems of Economic Dynamics and Planning* (Warsaw: PWN-Polish Scientific Publishers, 1964), 181–91.

"Stocks and Flows in the Theory of Interest," *The Theory of Interest Rates*, ed. F. H. Hahn and F. P. R. Brechling (London: Macmillan, 1965), 136–51.

"The Brookings – SSRC Quarterly Econometric Model of the US: Model Properties," with Gary Fromm, *American Economic Review, Papers and Proceedings*, LV, May 1965, 348–61.

"What Kind of Macro-Econometric Model for Developing Economies?" *Indian Economic Journal*, XIII, 1965, 313–24.

"On Econometric Models and Economic Policy," *The Oriental Economist*, XXXIV, June 1966, 375–8.

"Problems in the Estimation of Interdependent Systems," *Model Building in the Human Sciences*, ed. H. O. A. Wold (Monaco: Union Europeenne d'Editions, 1967), 51–8.

"Racial Patterns of Income and Employment in the USA," *Social and Economic Administration*, I, January 1967, 32–42.

"Some New Results in the Measurement of Capacity Utilization," with R. S. Preston, *American Economic Review*, LVII, March 1967, 34–58.

"Nonlinear Estimation of Aggregate Production Functions," with Ronald G. Bodkin, *Review of Economics and Statistics*, XLIX, February 1967, 28–44.

"On the Possibility of Another '29." *The Economic Outlook for 1967* (Ann Arbor, Michigan: University of Michigan Press, 1967), 45–87.

"Comment on Solving the Wharton Model," *Review of Economics and Statistics*, XLIX, November 1967, 647–51.

"Simultaneous Equation Estimation," *International Encyclopedia of the Social Sciences* (NY: Macmillan and Free Press, 1968), 281–94, vol. 14.

"Wage and Price Determination in Macroeconometrics," *Prices: Issues in Theory, Practice, and Public Policy*, ed. A. Phillips and O. E. Williamson (Philadelphia: University of Pennsylvania Press, 1967), 82–100.

"The Brookings Model Volume: A Review Article, A Comment," with G. Fromm, *Review of Economics and Statistics*, L, May 1968, 235-40.

"The Role of Mathematics in Economics," *The Mathematical Sciences*, COSRIMS (Cambridge, Mass.: MIT Press, 1969), 161-75.

"Stochastic Nonlinear Models," with R. S. Preston, *Econometrica*, 37, January 1969, 95-106.

"Estimation of Interdependent Systems in Macroeconometrics," *Econometrica*, 37, April 1969, 171-92.

"Econometric Model Building for Growth Projections," *Business Economics* IV, September 1969, 45-50.

"On the Possibility of the General Linear Economic Model," with D. W. Katzner, *Economic Models, Estimation, and Risk Programming*, ed. K. A. Fox, J. K. Sengupta, and G. V. L. Narasimham (Berlin: Springer-Verlag, 1969).

"Experience with Econometric Analysis of the U.S., Konjunktur Position," with M. K. Evans, *Is the Business Cycle Obsolete?*, ed. M. Bronfenbrenner (New York: Wiley-Interscience, 1969).

"Specification of Regional Econometric Models," *Papers of the Regional Science Association*, XXIII, 1969, 105-15.

"Nobel Laureates in Economics," *Science*, 166, November 7, 1969, 715-17.

"Estimation of Distributed Lags," with P. J. Dhrymes and K. Steiglitz, *International Economic Review*, XI, June 1970, 235-50.

"Econometric Growth Models for the Developing Economy," with J. Behrman, *Induction, Growth, and Trade*, ed. W. A. Eltis, M. F. G. Scott, J. N. Wolfe (Oxford: Clarendon Press, 1970).

"Forecasting and Policy Evaluation Using Large Scale Econometric Models: The State of the Art," *Frontiers of Quantitative Economics*, ed. M. D. Intriligator (Amsterdam: North-Holland, 1971).

"Estimating Effects within a Complete Econometric Model," with Paul Taubman, *Tax Incentives and Capital Spending*, ed. G. Fromm (Amsterdam: North-Holland, 1971).

"Wither Econometrics?," *Journal of the American Statistical Association*, 66, June 1971, 415-21.

"Empirical Evidence on Fiscal and Monetary Models," *Issues in Fiscal and Monetary Policy*, ed. J. J. Diamond (Chicago: DePaul University, 1971).

"The Role of War in the Maintenance of American Economic Prosperity," *Proceedings of the American Philosophical Society*, 115, December 30, 1971, 507-16.

"Guidelines in Economic Stabilization: A New Consideration," with Vijaya Duggal, *Wharton Quarterly*, VI, Summer 1971, 20-4.

"The Treatment of Expectations in Econometrics," *Uncertainty and Expectations in Economics*, ed. C. F. Carter and J. L. Ford (Oxford: Blackwell, 1972).

"The Survey: Lifeblood of the Quantitative Economist," *Survey of Current Business*, Anniversary Issue, 51, July 1971, Part II, 108-10.

"Short-Run Prediction and Long-Run Simulation of the Wharton Model," with M. K. Evans and M. Saito, *Econometric Models of Cyclical Behavior*, ed. B. G. Hickman (New York: Columbia University Press, 1972).

"Short- and Long-Term Simulations with the Brookings Model," with G. Fromm and G. R. Schink, *Econometric Models of Cyclical Behavior*, ed. B. G. Hickman (New York: Columbia University Press, 1972).

"Analog Solution of Econometric Models," with Hamid Habibagahi, *The Engineering Economist*, Vol. 17, No. 2, 1972, 115-33.

"Computerized Econometric Methods in Business Applications," *Journal of Contemporary Business*, Vol. 1, Spring, 1972, 63-71.

"Dynamic Properties of Nonlinear Econometric Models," with E. Phillip Howrey, *International Economic Review*, 13, October 1972, 599-618.

"Price Determination in the Wharton Model," *The Econometrics of Price Determination*, ed. Otto Eckstein (Washington: Federal Reserve Board, 1972), 221-36.

"Anticipations Variables in Macro-Econometric Models," with F. G. Adams, *Human Behavior in Economic Affairs*, ed. B. Strumpel *et al.* (Amsterdam: Elsevier, 1972).

"The Precision of Economic Prediction: Standards, Achievement, Potential," *The Economic Outlook for 1973* (Ann Arbor: University of Michigan Press, 1973), 91-111.

"The Wharton Forecast Record: A Self-Examination," with George R. Green, *The Wharton Quarterly*, Winter 1972-73, 22-8.

"The Treatment of Undersized Samples in Econometrics," *Econometric Studies of Macro and Monetary Relations*, ed. A. A. Powell and R. A. Williams (Amsterdam: North-Holland, 1973).

"Background, Organization, and Preliminary Results of Project LINK," with Bert Hickman and R. R. Rhomberg, *International Business Systems Perspectives*, ed. C. G. Alexandrides (Atlanta: Georgia State University, School of Business Administration, 1973).

"A Comparison of Eleven Econometric Models of the United States," with Gary Fromm, *American Economic Review*, Papers and Proceedings, LXIII, May 1973, 385-93.

"The Impact of Disarmament on Aggregate Economic Activity: An Econometric Analysis," with Kei Mori, *The Economic Consequences of Reduced Military Spending*, ed. B. Udis (Lexington, Mass.: D. C. Heath, 1973).

"Introduction," with B. G. Hickman and R. R. Rhomberg, *The International Linkage of National Economic Models*, ed. R. J. Ball (Amsterdam: North-Holland, 1973).

"Forecasting World Trade Within Project LINK," with A. Van Peeterssen, *The International Linkage of National Economic Models*, ed. R. J. Ball (Amsterdam: North-Holland, 1973).

"The Brookings Econometric Model: A Rational Perspective," with Gary Fromm, *Problems and Issues in Current Econometric Practice*, ed. Karl Brunner (Columbus: Ohio State University, 1972).

"Dynamic Analysis of Economic Systems," *International Journal of Mathe-*

matical Education in Science and Technology, 4, July–September, 1973, 341-59.

"Commentary on 'The State of the Monetarist Debate,'" *Federal Reserve Bank of St Louis Review*, 55, September 1973, 9-12.

"Capacity Utilization: Concept, Measurement, and Recent Estimates," with Virginia Long, *Brookings Papers on Economic Activity*, 3, 1973, 743-56.

"Issues in Econometric Studies of Investment Behavior," *Journal of Economic Literature*, XII, March 1974, 43-9.

"Notes on Testing the Predictive Performance of Econometric Models," with E. P. Howrey and M. D. McCarthy, *International Economic Review*, 15, June 1974, 366-83.

"LINK Model Simulations of International Trade: An Evaluation of the Effects of Currency Realignment," with K. Johnson, *Journal of Finance*, Papers and Proceedings, 29, May 1974, 617-30.

"Macroeconometric Model Building in Latin America: The Mexican Case," with Abel Beltran del Rio, *The Role of the Computer in Economic and Social Research in Latin America*, National Bureau of Economic Research (New York: Columbia University Press, 1974).

"Econometrics," *Encyclopaedia Britannica*, 15th ed., 1974.

"Supply Constraints in Demand Oriented Systems: An Interpretation of the Oil Crisis," *Zeitschrift für Nationalökonomie*, 34, 1974, 45-56.

"An Econometric Analysis of the Revenue and Expenditure Control Act of 1968-69," *Public Finance and Stabilization Policy*, ed. W. L. Smith and J. M. Culbertson (Amsterdam: North-Holland, 1974).

"Intractability of Inflation," *Methodology and Science*, vol. 7, 3, 1974, 156-73.

"The Wharton Mark III Model – A Modern IS-LM Construct," with M. D. McCarthy and Vijaya Duggal, *International Economic Review*, 15, October 1974.

"Estimation and Prediction in Dynamic Econometric Models," with H. N. Johnston and K. Shinjo, *Econometrics and Economic Theory*, ed. W. Sellekaerts (London: Macmillan, 1974).

"Stability in the International Economy: The LINK Experience," with Keith Johnson, *International Aspects of Stabilization Policies*, ed. A. Ando, R. Herring, R. Marston (Boston: Federal Reserve Bank of Boston, 1975).

"Research Contributions of the SSRC – Brookings Econometric Model Project – A Decade in Review," *The Brookings Model: Perspective and Recent Developments*, ed. Gary Fromm and Lawrence R. Klein (Amsterdam: North-Holland, 1975).

"The LINK Model of World Trade, with Application to 1972-73," with C. Moriguchi and A. Van Peeterssen, *International Trade and Finance*, ed. P. Kenen (Cambridge University Press, 1975).

"Long Term Policies and Outlook for World Inflation," *The Role of Japan in the Future World*, Proceedings of the 2nd Tsukuba International Symposium (University of Tsukuba, Japan, 1976), 99-110.

"The NBER/NSF Model Comparison Seminar: An Analysis of Results," with

Gary Fromm, *Annals of Economic and Social Measurement*, 5, Winter 1976, 1–28.

"Pacific Basin Econometric Research," *Central Bank Macroeconomic Modeling in Pacific Basin Countries* (San Francisco: Federal Reserve Bank of San Francisco, 1976).

"Five-Year Experience of Linking National Econometric Models and of Forecasting International Trade," *Quantitative Studies of International Economic Relations*, ed. H. Glejser (Amsterdam: North-Holland, 1976).

"Applications of the LINK System," with K. N. Johnson, J. Gana, M. Kurose, C. Weinberg, *The Models of Project LINK*, ed. J. Waelbroeck (Amsterdam: North-Holland, 1976).

"The Next Generation of Macro Models – The Present and Steps in Progress," *Proceedings of the Inaugural Convention of the Eastern Economic Association*, Albany, NY, October 25–7, 1974, 25–33.

"Early Warning Signals of Inflation," with S. A. Klein, *Economic Progress, Private Values, and Public Policy*, ed. B. Balassa and R. Nelson (Amsterdam: North-Holland, 1977).

"Statistical Needs for Economic Analysis: A User's Viewpoint," *Proceedings of the Business and Economic Statistics Section, American Statistical Association* (1976), 110–13.

"Intermediate Term Outlook for the Housing Market," with Vincent Su, *The Construction Industry: New Adaptations to a Changing Environment*, ed. W. Gomberg and L. M. Robbins (Philadelphia: Wharton Entrepreneurial Center, University of Pennsylvania, 1977).

"Project LINK," *The Columbia Journal of World Business*, XI, Winter 1976, 7–19; *Economics and Mathematical Methods*, XIII, May–June, 1977, 471–88, Acad. Sci. USSR (Russian), Lecture Series, 30, Center of Planning and Economic Research, Athens, 1977.

"Econometric Model Building at the Regional Level," with Norman J. Glickman, *Regional Science and Urban Economics*, 7, 1977, 3–23.

"Waiting for the Revival of Capital Formation," *The World Economy*, 1, October 1977, 35–46.

"Comments on Sargent and Sims' 'Business Cycle Modeling Without Pretending to Have Too Much *A Priori* Economic Theory,'" *New Methods in Business Cycle Research: Proceedings From a Conference*, ed. C. A. Sims (Minneapolis: Federal Reserve Bank of Minneapolis, 1977), 203–8.

"Econometrics of Inflation, 1965–1974: A Review of the Decade," *Analysis of Inflation: 1965–1974, Studies in Income and Wealth*, vol. 42, ed. J. Popkin (Cambridge: Ballinger for the National Bureau of Economic Research, 1977), 35–64.

"The Longevity of Economic Theory," *Quantitative Wirtschaftsforschung*, ed. Horst Albach *et al.* (Tubingen: J. C. B. Mohr, 1977), 411–19; reprinted in French, *Cahiers du Séminaire d'Économetrie*, No. 20 (CNRS, Paris), 1979.

"Economic Policy Formation Through the Medium of Econometric Models," *Frontiers of Quantitative Economics*, IIIB, ed. M. Intriligator (Amsterdam: North-Holland, 1977), 765–82.

"Comment on a Multiregional Input-Output Model of the World Economy," *The International Allocation of Economic Activity*, ed. B. Ohlin *et al.* (London: Macmillan, 1977), 531-7.

"The Deterrent Effect of Capital Punishment: An Assessment of the Estimates," with Brian Forst and Victor Filatov, *Deterrence and Incapacitation: Estimating the Effects of Criminal Sanctions on Crime Rates*, ed. A. Blumenstein *et al.* (Washington, DC: National Academy of Science, 1978), 336-60.

"Understanding Inflation," *Alternative Directions in Economic Policy*, ed. F. J. Bonello and T. R. Swartz (Notre Dame-London: University of Notre Dame Press, 1978), 62-77.

"Potentials of Econometrics for Commodity Stabilization Policy Analysis," *Stabilizing World Commodity Markets*, ed. F. G. Adams, S. A. Klein (Lexington, Mass.: Lexington Books, 1978), 105-16.

"The Supply Side," *American Economic Review*, 68, March 1978, 1-7.

"Computer Modeling of Macroeconomic Systems: The State of the Art," *Ökonometrische Modelle und Systeme*, ed. F. Schober and H. D. Plötzeneder (München: Oldenburg, 1978), 25-38 (videotape recording of lecture of December 10, 1975, Ottignies, Belgium).

"Oil and the World Economy," *Middle East Review*, X, Summer 1978, 21-8, and *Economic Impact*, No. 23, 1978/3, 49-55.

"Protectionism: An Analysis from Project LINK," with V. Su, *Journal of Policy Modeling*, January 1979, 5-35.

"Some Observations on the World Business Cycle," *International Cooperation and Stabilization Policies: A New Dimension of Keynesian Policy*, ed. L. R. Klein and C. Moriguchi (Tokyo: Forum for Policy Innovation, 1977), 4-16.

"Money in a General Equilibrium System: Empirical Aspects of the Quantity Theory," *Économie Appliquée*, XXXI, 1-2, 1978, 5-14.

"Trade Impact Studies Using the Wharton Annual and Industry Forecasting Model," *The Impact of International Trade and Investment on Employment*, ed. William G. Dewald (Washington, DC: US Department of Labor, Bureau of International Labor Affairs, 1978), 293-306.

"Perspectivas de la economia mundial, 1977-79," *Revista de Economia Latino-americana*, XIII, No. 52, 1978, 15-22.

"Disturbances to the International Economy," *After the Phillips Curve: Persistence of High Inflation and High Unemployment* (Federal Reserve Bank of Boston, 1979), 84-103.

"Econometrics," *Across the Board*, XVI, February 1979, 49-58.

"The Next Generation of Macro Models: The Present and Steps in Progress," *Communication and Control in Society*, ed. Klaus Krippendorff (New York: Gordon and Bresch, 1979), 293-303.

Transportation Demand – "Aggregate and Major Freight Category Demand Estimation," with Colin J. Loxley, *Forecasts of Freight System Demand and Related Research Needs* (Washington, DC: National Research Council, Assembly of Engineering, Committee on Transportation, 1979), 10-25.

Comment on: "An Overview of the Objectives and Framework of Seasonal

Adjustment" by Shirley Kallek, *Seasonal Analysis of Economic Time Series* (Washington, DC: Bureau of the Census, ER-1, 1978), 30-2.

"Political Aspects of Economic Control," *Theory for Economic Efficiency: Essays in Honor of Abba P. Lerner*, ed. Harry I. Greenfield *et al.* (Cambridge: MIT Press, 1979), 76-91.

"Managing the Modern Economy: Econometric Specification," *Optimal Control for Econometric Models: An Approach to Economic Policy Formulation*, ed. Sean Holly *et al.* (London: Macmillan, 1979), 265-85.

"Error Analysis of the LINK Model," with K. N. Johnson, *Modelling the International Transmission Mechanism*, ed. J. Sawyer (Amsterdam: North-Holland, 1979), 45-71.

"Long-Run Projections of the LINK World Trade Model," with Asher Tishler, *Modelling the International Transmission Mechanism*, ed. J. Sawyer (Amsterdam: North-Holland, 1979), 73-94.

"Coordination of International Fiscal Policies and Exchange Rate Revaluations," with Vincent Su and Paul Beaumont, *Modelling the International Transmission Mechanism*, ed. J. Sawyer (Amsterdam: North-Holland, 1979), 143-59.

"Demand Forecasting and Capacity Creation in the Private Sector I," *Long-Term Economic Planning*, ed. P. K. Mitra (Laxenburg, Austria: IIASA, 1978), 41-59.

"Ökonometrische Modelle: Empirische Anwendung," *Handwörterbuch der mathematischen Wirtschaftswissenschaften, Ökonometrie und Statistik*, ed. Günter Menges (Wiesbaden: Gabler, 1978), 105-18.

"Direct Estimates of Unemployment Rate and Capacity Utilization in Macroeconometric Models," with Vincent Su, *International Economic Review*, 20, October 1979, 725-40.

"International Coordination of Economic Policies," with H. Georgiadis and V. Su, *Greek Economic Review*, I, August 1979, 27-47.

"Regional Sublinkages of Economic Systems," *Proceedings of the Fourth Pacific Basin Central Bank Conference on Econometric Modeling* (Tokyo: Bank of Japan, 1980), 3-18.

"International Research Cooperation," *Man, Environment, Space and Time*, I, Fall 1979, 47-51.

"Recent Economic Fluctuations and Stabilization Policies: An Optimal Control Approach," with Vincent Su, *Quantitative Economics and Development*, ed. L. R. Klein, M. Nerlove, and S. C. Tsiang (New York: Academic Press, 1980), 225-54.

"Use of Econometric Models in the Policy Process," *Economic Modeling*, ed. Paul Ormerod (London: Heinemann, 1980), 309-29.

"Money Supply Hard to Control," *Controlling Money: A Discussion*, Intro. W. R. Allen (Los Angeles: International Institute for Economic Research, 1980), 9-14; 39-42.

"On Econometric Models," *Issues and Current Studies*, The National Research Council, 1980 (Washington, DC: National Academy of Sciences, 1981), 41-55.

"Tax Policies and Economic Expansion in the U.S.," *Technology in Society*, 3, 1981, 205-12.

"Oil Prices and the World Economy," *The Middle East Challenge*, ed. Thomas Naff (Carbondale: Southern Illinois University Press, 1981), 75-85.

"The LINK Project," *International Trade and Multi-Country Models*, ed. R. Courbis (Paris: Economica, 1981), 197-209.

"Some Economic Scenarios for the 1980s" (Nobel Memorial Lecture, 8 December 1980), *Les Prix Nobel* (Stockholm: Almqvist & Wiksell, 1980), 273-94.

"Project LINK: Policy Implications for the World Economy," *Knowledge and Power in a Global Society*, ed. William M. Evan (Beverly Hills: Sage, 1981), 91-106.

"The Practice of Macro-Econometric Model Building and Its Rationale," with E. P. Howrey, M. D. McCarthy, and G. R. Schink, *Large Scale Macro-Econometric Models*, ed. J. Kmenta and J. Ramsey (Amsterdam: North-Holland, 1981), 19-58.

"Scale of Macro-Econometric Models and Accuracy of Forecasting," with G. Fromm, *Large Scale Macro-Econometric Models*, ed. J. Kmenta and J. Ramsey (Amsterdam: North-Holland, 1981), 369-88.

"Computers in Economics," "Econometrics," "Economic Models," *Encyclopedia of Economics*, ed. Douglas Greenwald (New York: McGraw-Hill, 1981), 303-8.

"Equazione per il futuro," *Revista IBM*, XVII, 3, 1981, 5-11.

"The Neoclassical Tradition of Keynesian Economics and the Generalized Model," *Samuelson and Neoclassical Economics*, ed. G. R. Feiwel (Boston: Klerwer-Nijhoff, 1982), 244-62.

"The Value of Models in Policy Analysis," *Modeling Agriculture for Policy Analysis in the 1980s* (Kansas City: Federal Reserve Bank of Kansas City, 1982), 1-18.

"International Aspects of Industrial Policy," *Toward a New U.S. Industrial Policy*, ed. M. L. and S. M. Wachter (Philadelphia: University of Pennsylvania Press, 1981).

"Coordinated Monetary Policy and the World Economy," with R. Simes and P. Voisin, *Prévision et Analyse Économique*, 2, July-October, 1981, 75-105.

"Purchasing Power Parity in Medium Term Simulation of the World Economy," with V. Filatov and S. Fardoust, *Scandinavian Journal of Economics*, 1981, 479-96.

"The World Economy – A Global Model," with Peter Pauly and Pascal Voisin, *Perspectives in Computing*, 2, May 1982, 4-17.

'The Scholarly Foundations of the Econometrics Industry," *Economics and the World Around It*, ed. S. H. Hymans (Ann Arbor: University of Michigan Press, 1982), 111-22.

"Industrial Policy in the World Economy: Medium Term Simulations," with C. A. B. Bollino and S. Fardoust, *Journal of Policy Modeling*, 4 (2), 1982, 175-89.

Index

163